Microsoft®
Money2000

GW00728009

PUBLISHED BY
Microsoft Press
A Division of Microsoft Corporation
One Microsoft Way
Redmond, Washington 98052-6399

Library of Congress Cataloging-in-Publication Data
Nelson, Stephen L., 1959-
    Microsoft Money 2000 At a Glance / Stephen L. Nelson.
      p. cm.
    Includes index.
    ISBN 0-7356-0811-3
    1. Microsoft Money.   2. Finance, Personal--Computer programs.
3. Investments--Computer programs. I. Title. II. Title: Microsoft
Money two thousand At a Glance.
HG179.N426149   1999
332.024'00285'5369--dc21   99-33880
                                        CIP

Printed and bound in the United States of America.

1 2 3 4 5 6 7 8 9 WCWC   4 3 2 1 0 9

Distributed in Canada by Penguin Books Canada Limited.

A CIP catalogue record for this book is available from the British Library.

Microsoft Press books are available through booksellers and distributors worldwide. For further information about international editions, contact your local Microsoft Corporation office or contact Microsoft Press International directly at fax (425) 936-7329. Visit our Web site at mspress.microsoft.com.

Microsoft, Microsoft Press, the Microsoft Press logo, MoneyCentral, MSN, and Outlook are either registered trademarks or trademarks of Microsoft Corporation in the United States and/or other countries. Other product and company names mentioned herein may be the trademarks of their respective owners.

The example companies, organizations, products, people, and events depicted herein are fictitious. No association with any real company, organization, product, person, or event is intended or should be inferred.

For Stephen L. Nelson, Inc.
Writers: Steve Nelson and Kaarin Dolliver
Copy Editor: Paula Thurman
Technical Editor: Jason Gerend

For Microsoft Press
Acquisitions Editor: Christey Bahn
Project Editor: Kim Fryer

Contents

"How do I set up a new Money file?"

see page 8

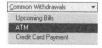

Record an ATM withdrawal
see page 23

Filter the information
included in a report or chart
see page 61

"How can I use
Money to
estimate my
income and
capital gains
taxes?"

see page 92

"How do I download the current prices in my portfolio from the Internet?"

see page 120

Maximum Gain

Minimum Gain

First Acquired

Specify lots to sell
see page 124

"How do I record depreciation and capital improvements on real estate investments?"

see pages 144–45

Number: ✉3001

Send an electronic payment
see page 160

11 **Managing a Small Business with Money** **173**

Index **203**

"How do I track employee withholdings?"

see page 189

About This Book

Microsoft Money 2000 At a Glance is for anyone who wants to exploit the power of Microsoft's personal finance manager, Money 2000. I think you'll find this book to be a straightforward, easy-to-read, and easy-to-use reference tool. Based on the premise that it's tough to make "smart" decisions about money, this book's purpose is to help you use your computer as a tool to better organize and manage your financial affairs.

No Computerese!

Let's face it—when there's a task you don't know how to do but you need to get it done in a hurry, or when you're stuck in the middle of a task and can't figure out what to do next, there's nothing more frustrating than having to read page after page of technical background material. You want the information you need—nothing more, nothing less—and you want it now! And the information should be easy to find and understand.

That's what this book is all about. It's written in plain English—no technical jargon and no computerese. No single task in the book takes more than two pages. Just look up the task in the index or the table of contents, turn to the page, and there it is. The task itself is laid out step by step and accompanied by a graphics image that adds visual clarity. Just read the introduction, follow the steps, look at the illustrations, and get your work done with a minimum of hassle.

You may want to turn to another task if the one you're working on has a "See Also" in the left column. Because there's a lot of overlap among tasks, I didn't want to keep repeating myself; you might find more elementary or more advanced tasks laid out on the pages referenced. I've also added some useful tips here and there and offered a "Try This" once in a while to give you a context in which to use the task. But by and large, I've tried to remain true to the heart and soul of the book, which is that the information you need should be available to you *at a glance*.

What's New

If you're looking for what's new in Money 2000, just look for this new icon **New**2000 inserted throughout the book. You'll find the new icon in the table of contents so you can quickly and easily identify new or improved features in Money. You'll also find the new icon on the first page of each section. There it will serve as a handy reminder of the latest improvements in Money as you move from one task to another.

Useful Tasks...

Whether you use Money to track several investment portfolios or simply to help keep your checkbook, I've tried to pack this book with procedures for everything I could think of that you might want to do, from the simplest tasks to some of the more esoteric ones.

...And the Easiest Way to Do Them

Another thing I've tried to do in *Microsoft Money 2000 At a Glance* is to find and document the easiest way to accomplish a task. Money 2000 often provides many ways to obtain a single result, which can be daunting or delightful, depending on the way you like to work. If you tend to stick with one favorite and familiar approach, the methods described in this book are the way to go. If you prefer to try out alternative techniques, go ahead! The intuitiveness of Money invites exploration, and you're likely to discover ways of doing things that you think are easier or that you like better. If you do, that's great! It's exactly what the creators of Money had in mind when they provided so many alternatives.

A Quick Overview

You don't have to read this book in any particular order. The book is designed so that you can jump in, get the information you need, and then close the book, keeping it near your computer until the next time you need it. But that doesn't mean I scattered the information about with wild abandon. If you were to read the book from front to back, you'd find a logical progression from the simple tasks to the more complex ones. Here's a quick overview.

Section 2 introduces Money, explains how you can begin using Money, and describes some Money basics that you'll want to know as you begin exploring this useful tool.

If you're brand new to accounting software, you'll want to review Sections 3 and 4, which describe everything you need to know about using Money's account registers to keep track of your basic accounts. Section 3 describes how you use Money to keep track of your bank accounts, and Section 4 describes how you use Money to monitor credit card accounts.

Sections 5 and 6 contain a wealth of information useful to all levels of Money users. Section 5 explains Money's Report and Chart feature. It talks in depth about the different kinds of reports and charts you can create, and why and when you would want to create some of the more common reports. Section 6 describes how you use the tools in Money 2000 Deluxe to build a budget, plan for the future, and track income and deductions for taxes.

Sections 7, 8, and 9 describe different types of specialized accounts you might want to create and use if you have loans, liabilities, investments, or assets you want Money to help you track. Section 7 describes how you can use Money to track your assets and liabilities. It goes through the different kinds of transactions you make in loan and liability accounts and provides several tips and strategies for getting out of debt. Sections 8 and 9 describe how you can use Money to track your investments. Section 8 deals with mutual funds, stocks, and bonds, and Section 9 deals with passive and active real estate investments.

If you have an Internet connection, you'll definitely want to review Section 10, which describes how you can use Money to retrieve your bank statements online and how to make electronic payments. This section discusses how to set up online banking and bill payment services with participating banks, and also discusses where you can find financial advice on the Internet.

The remaining section of this book delves into a more advanced topic. Section 11 discusses how you can use Money to keep track of small business finances. You'll need to read this section only if you have a small business and want to use Money to help with your business accounting. This section describes such things as invoicing, accounts receivable accounting, and preparing payroll.

A Final Word (or Two)

Let me close this introductory section with some final comments that I hope you'll find helpful and encouraging as you use this book and learn Money. I had three goals in writing this book. I want this book to help you:

◆ Do all the things you want to do with Money 2000.

◆ Discover how to do things you didn't know you wanted to do with Money.

◆ Enjoy using Money.

My "thank you" for buying this book is the achievement of those goals. I hope you'll have as much fun using *Microsoft Money 2000 At a Glance* as I've had writing it. The best way to learn is by doing, and that's what I hope you'll get from this book.

Jump right in!

2

The Basics of Money

G etting started with Microsoft Money 2000 is very easy because you don't need much prior computer knowledge to begin using the program. That said, let me suggest that you'll benefit by having a little friendly help starting out and navigating your way through Money for the first time. This way, you'll get up and running more quickly, you'll get the feel for Money's general organization, and you won't make simple mistakes that cause you to waste time later or miss out on some neat benefit.

Don't worry if you're not an expert on personal finance, budgeting, or investments. Of course, it helps if you know something about these topics, but this knowledge isn't re-quired to make good use of Money. As you read through this book or flip to a page for help with a specific task, you'll find financial tips and definitions of terms to help you out.

Getting Started with Money

To use Money, you first need to install it. If you're not sure whether Money is installed, click the Start button and then choose Programs. If you see Microsoft Money 2000 listed, the program is already installed. If you don't see it, follow the steps on this page to install Money 2000.

TIP

Install another way. *If the Installation Wizard For Microsoft Money 2000 dialog box doesn't appear on your screen when you insert the Money CD-ROM in your CD-ROM drive, you can install Money the same way you install other Microsoft Windows applications—use the Add/Remove Programs tool in Control Panel.*

Install Money

1. Insert the Money 2000 CD-ROM in your CD-ROM drive to start the Microsoft Money 2000 Installation Wizard.

2. Click Next to start the Setup program.

3. Close any programs you have running, and click Continue to continue with the setup.

4. Click the large button to install Money in the location it suggests.

5. When Money has completed copying files, click Yes if you want to place a shortcut to Money on your desktop.

6. Click OK when the installation is complete.

Install Microsoft Internet Explorer. *The Money Setup program searches your computer for Internet Explorer 5. Money 2000 requires Internet Explorer 5. If the Setup program detects that you don't have Internet Explorer 5 on your computer, it asks you to install it.*

Upgrade Money. *If you're upgrading from a previous version of Money, Money 2000 asks whether you want to update your Money file to Money 2000. You probably want to do this so you can continue working with the data you've already entered in Money.*

Collect your data. *When you first set up your Money file, it helps to have your financial information handy so you can enter it at one time. So you may want to gather your last paycheck stubs and your last bank statements, information on investments or loans you have, and your last regular bills.*

Easy installation. *You can install and run Money 2000 Standard, Money 2000 Deluxe, and Money 2000 Business & Personal in the same way.*

Run Money

1 Click the Start button.

2 Choose Programs.

3 Choose Microsoft Money 2000.

4 Click Start Here to create a new Money file. Money displays the main page of the Money Setup Assistant. Click buttons to go through the tasks involved in setting up Money.

5 When Money displays forms, fill in information about yourself, your finances, and how you intend to use Money to tailor the program to your needs.

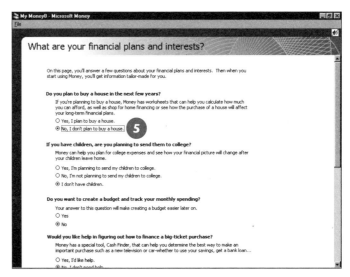

Creating and Opening Money Files

After you've set up a Money file, the first screen you'll see is the Money Home Page. At this point, you're ready to begin setting up new accounts in the file, opening existing accounts, or importing accounts from Quicken.

Open a Money File

1. Choose Open from the File menu.

2. Click the down arrow in the Look In drop-down list box, and locate the drive or folder in which your Money file is stored.

3. Double-click the Money file when you find it.

Create a Money File

1. Choose New from the File menu, and then choose New File from the submenu.

2. Enter a name for the file in the File Name box, and click OK.

3. Money creates the new file and displays the Money Setup Assistant.

4. Use the Money Setup Assistant to tell Money about yourself and the options you want in the file you're creating.

Create separate files. *You need to create a separate Money file for each business whose finances you want to track using Money. You might also want to let older children have their own separate Money files so they can learn to track their accounts and spending and develop good saving habits.*

The default storage location. *By default, Money saves the Money files you create in the My Documents folder, a good place for them.*

Back up an open file. *If you have a file open when you tell Money that you want to create a new file or open another file, Money prompts you to back up the currently open file. This is because Money can display only one file at a time. Click Back Up Now to back up to your floppy drive, or click Options to store the backup copy in a different location.*

Import a File from Quicken

1. Choose Convert Quicken File from the File menu.

2. Click the down arrow in the Look In drop-down list box, and locate the drive and folder in which your Quicken file is stored. The default folder for your Quicken files is the Quickenw folder.

3. Double-click the Quicken file when you find it to start the Converter Wizard For Quicken, and click Next to continue.

4. Money suggests a name and storage location for the new Money file it will create from your Quicken file. You can change the name if you want, but keep the file stored wherever Money suggests and click Next to begin converting the files.

5. Click Finish.

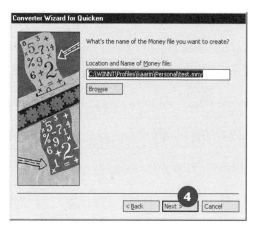

The Money Home Page

Click here to return to the Money Home Page.

Click here to alternately display an account register or to view all your accounts in the Accounts Place.

Click here to move backward through the windows you've recently visited.

Click here to display Advisor FYI alerts, financial news, and the chart of the day.

Click here to personalize your Home Page.

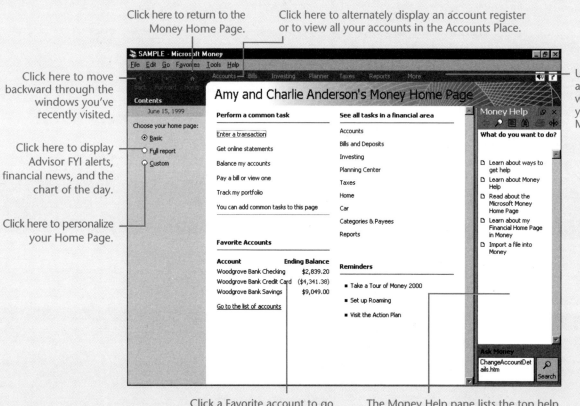

Use the navigation bar at the top of every window to navigate your way through Money.

Click a Favorite account to go to that account's register.

The Money Help pane lists the top help topics for the area you're viewing.

Getting Help in Money

If you have questions about how something works in Money, you can access help in several ways.

Use the Money Help Pane

1 If you don't see the Money Help pane on the right side of the Money window, click the question mark button.

2 Use one of the following methods to get help:

- Click the Contents toolbar button to see Money Help's table of contents. To view information on a topic, click the topic-heading hyperlink.

- Click the Keyword Search toolbar button to find a word or phrase in Money Help. Type a word or double-click a word in the list to display a list of related help topics. To display the text of a topic, click its hyperlink in the list.

- Click the New Search toolbar button to ask Help a question and to display the top five help topics for the area you're currently viewing. Enter your question in the Ask Money box, and click Search. To learn more about a topic, click its hyperlink.

New Search

Contents

Keyword Search

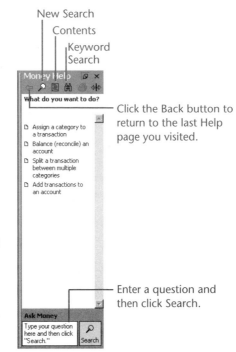

Click the Back button to return to the last Help page you visited.

Enter a question and then click Search.

Archiving Money Files

Over time you'll probably find that your accounts fill up quickly with dozens of transactions. After a year or so, you may want to rid your Money file of old transactions to make your accounts quicker and easier to work with. To do this, you create an archive file by removing selected transactions from selected accounts. By archiving your Money file, you still maintain old records; you just move them to another file to streamline your current Money file.

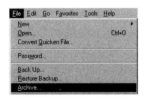

Archive a Money File

1 Choose Archive from the File menu.

2 Enter the cut-off date before which you want specified transactions removed.

3 Click OK.

4 Enter a name for the archive file, or accept the default name. Do not change the storage location that Money suggests.

5 Click OK.

6 Tell Money which types of files you want removed from each of your Money accounts by selecting options for each account and clicking OK to proceed to the next account.

Backing Up Your Data

As soon as you start using Money, you'll want to begin backing up the financial information you collect. This practice ensures that you'll have a copy of your financial records in case the originals are destroyed or corrupted.

Back Up a Money File

1. Choose Back Up from the File menu.

2. Specify where you want to store the backup copy of your file:

   ◆ To back up your file to a floppy disk, click the Back Up To Floppy option button and select the floppy drive holding the disk on which you want to place the backup file.

   ◆ To back up your file to a hard drive, select the Back Up To Hard Disk option button and click Browse to tell Money where you want to store the backup copy.

3. If you're backing up your Money file to your hard disk, use the Backup dialog box's Save In drop-down list box to specify the disk and folder location for the file and click OK.

4. Click Backup Now to back up the file to the location you specified.

2

Keeping Your Checkbook

At its core, Microsoft Money 2000 is a computerized checkbook. Instead of keeping track of your checks and deposits in a paper register, you use an on-screen register. You get several important benefits from computerizing your checkbook records:

◆ Your computer calculates your account balances so that as long as you enter the correct numbers, your account balance is correct.

◆ You can describe checks as falling into specific income and expense categories. That way, you can find out how much you spend in a certain category with just a couple of mouse clicks.

◆ You can reconcile your account in roughly two minutes.

◆ You can print checks or transmit payments electronically, which makes paying bills much easier and much quicker.

Setting Up Bank Accounts

To use Money, you set up an account for each bank account you want to track. Then you open the register and record the checks you write and the deposits you make for each account. Money doesn't change the way you record checks and deposits; it simply provides an on-screen form for you to use instead of a paper register.

⊟ **Bank Accounts**

Woodgrove Bank Checking

Woodgrove Bank Savings

SEE ALSO

See "Setting Up Online Services" on pages 154–155 for information on setting up accounts for online services.

TIP

Online services not available. *Money asks you whether you want to set up online services or create more accounts at the same bank only if you entered the name of your bank in step 3.*

Create an Account

1. Click Accounts on the navigation bar, and then click Set Up Accounts in the left pane.

2. Click the Add A New Account hyperlink.

3. Enter the name of your bank or select it from the drop-down list, and click Next.

4. Verify that the correct bank is selected, and click Next.

5. Select either Checking, Savings, or Bank from the list, and click Next.

6. Type a name for your account or accept the default that Money provides, and click Next.

7. Enter your account number if you know it, and click Next.

8. Enter the ending balance from your last bank statement, and click Next.

9. If you don't want to set up any more accounts for the moment, click the I Have No Other Accounts At This Institution option button, and click Next.

10. Click Finish.

TIP

Transaction options. *This book shows how to use transaction forms to enter transactions in an account register. You can switch between entering transactions directly in a register and using transaction forms by selecting or clearing the Show Transaction Forms check box.*

TIP

Add favorite accounts. *If you use an account frequently, select it as a favorite so you can access it quickly. After you select an account as a favorite, it appears on the Money Home Page and directly on the Accounts menu in the left pane.*

TIP

Edit favorite accounts. *To edit your list of favorite accounts, click Set Up Accounts in the left pane. Then click the Pick Favorite Accounts hyperlink.*

Open an Account Register

1 Click Accounts on the navigation bar.

2 Click the account's hyperlink.

3 To switch to a different account register, click Accounts in the left pane and choose the account from the menu.

Add an Account to Your Favorites List

1 With the account's register displayed, click Change Account Details in the left pane.

2 Select the Favorite Account check box.

Storing Additional Account Information

You can easily store additional information about all the accounts you create. You can store notes about interest rates, minimum balance requirements, and transaction fees.

Other Tasks:
Find a transaction
Analyze spending ▶
Change account details

TIP

Edit an account setup. *You can also use the Update Details window to edit the account setup. For example, you can edit the name of the account or the opening balance.*

Store Information About Your Bank Account

1 Display the account register.

2 Click Change Account Details in the left pane to display the Update Details window for the account.

3 Use the Comment field to write notes to yourself, such as a reminder about fees you want to avoid.

4 Select an account purpose that best corresponds to the way you use the account from the Budget Group drop-down list box.

5 Enter the minimum balance in the Minimum Balance field.

Recording Income

When you enter transactions in a register, you use the transaction forms at the bottom of the Account Register window. Click the tab you want to use, and then describe the deposit or withdrawal by filling in the fields. To move between the fields, press the Tab key or use the mouse to click the field you want. Click Enter to record your transaction and recalculate the balance.

TIP

Don't record bank interest earned. *You don't need to record an income transaction for interest earned on your bank account. You do this when you reconcile the account.*

TIP

Record a cash-back deposit. *To record a deposit with cash back, click Common Deposits in the transaction form and choose Deposit With Cash Back from the menu. Categorize the deposit, enter the deposit and cash back amounts, and then click OK.*

Record a Deposit

1. In the bank account's register, click the Deposit tab. If the Deposit tab is currently displayed, click New.

2. Optionally, enter a deposit number or check number in the Number field.

3. Enter the deposit date.

4. Enter the name of the person or business that is paying you.

5. Enter the amount of the deposit.

6. Select an income category and subcategory to describe the deposit.

7. Enter a memo for the deposit.

8. Click Enter.

3

Using the Paycheck Wizard

As you well know, a certain amount of your paycheck is deducted right off the top of your earnings each and every time your employer pays you. Even though this money never actually makes it into your hands, Money can help you keep track of these deductions. Money can help you monitor how much you pay in federal, state, and local income taxes, how much you are paying for health insurance, and how much you put in employer 401(k) plans.

```
Transfer : Woodgrove Bank Credit Card
Transfer : Woodgrove Bank Savings
Paycheck
Loan Payment : Car Loan
Loan Payment : Home Loan
Credit Card Payment : Woodgrove Bank
```

Record a Paycheck

1 In the bank account's register, click the Deposit tab. If the Deposit tab is currently displayed, click New.

2 Enter the paycheck number in the Number field.

3 Enter the deposit date.

4 Enter the name of your employer in the From field.

5 Enter the word *Paycheck* in the Category field, and press the Tab key to start the Paycheck Wizard.

6 If Money asks whether you want to track your taxes and deductions, click Yes and then click Next to continue.

7 If Money displays a series of dialog boxes asking whether part of the paycheck is automatically deposited into a retirement or savings account, select the appropriate options and specify into which accounts these deductions are deposited. Click Next to proceed through the wizard, and then click Next to display the Paycheck dialog box.

Employer retirement accounts. *If you have a tax-deferred retirement account through your employer, you can set up a Money account for it in the Paycheck Wizard by typing a name for the retirement account when Money asks. A retirement account works the same way as a regular investment account, so refer to Section 8 for more information about working with a retirement account.*

8 On the Wages tab, enter your gross wages.

9 On the Deductions Before Taxes tab, enter tax-deductible contributions to a retirement account.

10 On the Taxes tab, specify how much you paid in income tax, Social Security, and Medicare.

11 On the Deductions After Taxes tab, enter any post-tax contributions to a savings account.

12 Click Done, and the Paycheck Wizard enters the paycheck amount in the Amount field.

13 Enter a note (such as the pay period or job) in the Memo field.

14 Click Enter to record the paycheck.

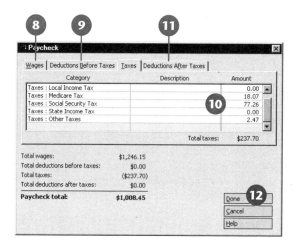

Recording Expenses

Recording expenses works in much the same way as recording income. The only real difference is which transaction form you use.

SEE ALSO

See "Assigning Transactions to Multiple Categories" on page 29 for information on how to record a check that falls into more than one category.

TIP

Create new categories. *If you can't find a category that adequately describes an income or expense, you can create a new category by entering it in the Category field. When you click Enter, Money displays a dialog box that asks you to name and describe the category. You can also create subcategories within categories in the same way.*

Record a Check

1 In the bank account's register, click the Withdrawal tab. If the Withdrawal tab is currently displayed, click New.

2 Click Common Withdrawals, and choose Write A Check from the menu.

3 Enter the check number, or type *P* for Print.

4 Enter the check date.

5 Enter the name of the person or business you're paying.

6 Enter the check amount.

7 Select an expense category and subcategory to describe the check.

8 Click Enter to record the check.

Record debit card transactions. *To record debit card purchases, click Common Withdrawals in the Withdrawal transaction form and choose Debit Card Purchase from the menu. Money enters the word* Debit *in the Number field of the Withdrawal transaction form. If you choose Debit Card Purchase With Cash Back from the menu, Money displays a dialog box you can use to categorize the purchase and enter the purchase and cash back amounts. Click OK to continue filling out the Withdrawal transaction form.*

Record an ATM Withdrawal

1. In the bank account's register, click the Withdrawal tab. If the Withdrawal tab is currently displayed, click New.

2. Click Common Withdrawals, and choose ATM from the menu. Choose an amount from the submenu to enter that amount in the transaction form and categorize the withdrawal according to a previous cash withdrawal, or choose Other Amount to enter the amount and category manually.

3. Enter a reference or serial number for the withdrawal.

4. Enter the withdrawal date.

5. Enter the withdrawal amount.

6. Select an expense category and subcategory to describe the withdrawal.

7. Enter a memo to describe the withdrawal.

8. Click Enter to record the withdrawal.

Printing Checks

You don't need to print your checks with Money, but many users do. The idea is that you save time—and produce neater check forms—by doing so. When you choose to print checks, Money uses the information that you enter when you record your checks.

Describe a Check to Be Printed

1. When you enter a check in a register, type the letter *P* in the Number field. If you haven't recorded the payee's address in Money before, Money displays a dialog box asking for it after you finish writing the check.

2. If you're sending the check through the mail in a window envelope, enter the payee's address.

3. Click OK.

4. Click Enter to record the check.

Set Up Your Printer for Printing Checks

1. Choose Print Setup from the File menu, and choose Check Setup from the submenu.

2. Select the printer on which you want to print the checks.

3. Select the type of check form you're using.

4. If you use a specific tray for loading check forms, select the printer tray in the Source field.

5. Click OK.

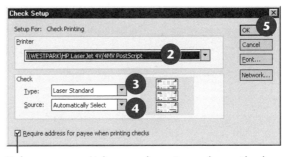

Unless you use window envelopes to send your checks, clear the Require Address For Payee When Printing Checks box. You don't always need to enter the payee's address when you print a check.

Which way's up? *If you're unsure about which way to load the check forms in your printer, test it by writing the words* Left *and* Right *on a blank piece of paper and then printing a dummy check on this paper. You might even want to keep this dummy check as a reference.*

Prevent check forgery. *It's a good practice to carefully sign your checks using a signature that isn't easily duplicated. Signatures that consist of just a wavy line and some squiggles are more easily forged. Also remember to write the word* VOID *in large letters across the face of any check that is incorrectly printed or written.*

Print a Check

1. Display the checking account register.

2. Click Print Checks in the left pane. (This link appears only after you've described a check you want to print.)

3. To print specific checks, click the Selected Checks option button.

4. Select the checks you want to print in the Select Checks dialog box, and then click OK.

5. Look at the preprinted number of your first check form, and enter this number in the Number Of First Check In Printer field.

6. Load the appropriate number of checks in your printer, and click Print. Money prints your computer checks.

7. If the computer checks printed correctly, click Finish. If they didn't, click Reprint.

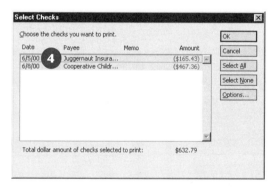

Entering Transactions in Other Currencies

If you withdraw money or make a purchase in another country, you can use Money's Currency Converter to convert the amount you spend into your local currency.

TIP

Find exchange rates. *You may be able to get the exchange rate from the newspaper, or you may need to get it from your statement because exchange rates (and fees) vary depending on the type of transaction.*

TRY THIS

Update exchange rates. *To update currency exchange rates online, choose Options from the Tools menu and click the Currencies tab. Select the exchange rate you want to update and how you want it described, and select the Update Exchange Rate Online check box. The next time you connect to the Internet, Money downloads exchange-rate updates.*

Use the Currency Converter

1. When you record the transaction, enter the amount you spent in the foreign currency in the Amount field.

2. While still in the Amount field, press the F8 key to open the Currency Converter.

3. Select the foreign currency from which you want to convert.

4. Select an option for how you want to specify the exchange rate.

5. Enter the exchange rate for the day that the transaction took place.

6. Click OK. Money enters the corresponding amount of your local currency in the Amount field.

Timesaving Tips for Entering Transactions

◆ You can enter transactions directly in the register without using transaction forms (the tabs at the bottom of the Account Register window) by clicking the View down arrow and choosing Enter Transactions Directly Into The Register. Then click the View down arrow again, and choose All Transaction Details so that you can enter category and memo descriptions directly into the register as well.

◆ AutoComplete remembers every transaction you make, and if it recognizes a payee name as you're typing, it fills in the rest of the name for you so that you don't have to keep typing. If AutoComplete is correct, just press the Tab key to have it fill out the rest of the check for you. (You can change the check amount or any of the other fields if necessary.) If you don't want to accept the match AutoComplete finds, just continue typing.

Pay to: Springfield Airlines

◆ Money 2000 recognizes over 700,000 companies and AutoCategorizes transactions for these companies. For example, if you enter the name of a well-known gas station, fast-food restaurant, or hotel chain in the Pay To field, Money suggests a category for the transaction.

◆ If you want to enter a memo to yourself that you don't want to appear on a printed check or an online payment, just put the memo inside curly brackets ({}) in the Pay To field.

Pay to: Sean Chai {Karin's teacher}

◆ To enter today's date in the Date field, type Ctrl+D. Type a plus sign (+) to go to the next day or a minus sign (-) to go to the previous day.

◆ AutoComplete by default enters the next check number if you tell it you want to record another check. Click the plus sign (+) to go to the following number or the minus sign (-) to go to the previous number.

◆ Click the down arrow in the Date field to enter a date using the Calendar. Click the arrows at the sides of the month to go forward or backward through the months to find a date; then click the date to enter it in the Date field.

◆ If you need to add, subtract, multiply, or divide numbers to get a deposit or withdrawal amount, click the down arrow beside the Amount field to display the Calculator. Click the numbers and operators, and then click = to calculate the amount.

Recording Transfers

There's a good chance that you have both a checking account and a savings account. If this is the case, you should know how to record one other type of bank account transaction, an account transfer. This works pretty much like you'd expect: you need to identify the accounts you're moving money between, the date of the transfer, and the amount of the transfer.

$1,000.00 to Woodgrove Bank Credit Card
$537.73 to Woodgrove Bank Credit Card
$3,500.00 to Fergusson & Bardell Inves (Cash)
$751.77 to Woodgrove Bank Credit Card
$1,236.02 to Woodgrove Bank Credit Card

SEE ALSO

See "Transferring Money Online" on page 166 for more information about transferring money electronically with online banking.

Record a Transfer

1. In an account register, click the Transfer tab. If the Transfer tab is currently displayed, click New.

2. Select the account from which you're moving funds.

3. Enter the transfer date.

4. Select the account to which you're moving the funds.

5. Enter the transfer amount.

6. Leave the Pay To field empty.

7. Optionally, enter a note in the Memo field.

8. Click Enter to record the transfer and recalculate the balance for both accounts.

Assigning Transactions to Multiple Categories

If you're a frequent "one-stop shopper," you'll often find that a single check you write falls into several categories. Fortunately, Money lets you split transactions into different categories. For example, maybe you wrote a check to a local grocery store, but the check didn't pay for just one thing. You bought some groceries. You had a drug prescription filled. And you bought some flowers for a friend's birthday. Money makes it easy to record this check in three spending categories.

TIP

Add a category. *You can add a new category or subcategory to the Categories list by typing it in the Category or Subcategory box.*

Split a Transaction Between Categories

1 Click Split in the Withdrawal or Deposit transaction form.

2 Enter the first category and subcategory on the first line.

3 Optionally, enter a memo to describe the first spending category. For example, you might want to list exactly what you bought.

4 Enter the amount spent or received in the first category in the Amount field.

5 Repeat steps 3 through 5 on the second and subsequent lines for each spending category and subcategory.

6 Click Done when you finish. Money returns you to the account register transaction form so you can continue filling out your transaction.

Working with Lists

You use the Categories & Payees area to work with your lists of categories and payees. Using these lists, you can add, delete, and move categories and payees. For example, if an individual or a company changes its name, you can change the name in the Payees list to reflect it. You can also merge payees if you find you have more than one spelling of the same name.

TIP

Edit a category. *Select a category from the Categories list and click Modify to rename a category or to change it from an expense category to an income category (or vice versa).*

Move a Category

1 Click More on the navigation bar, and choose Categories & Payees from the menu.

2 Select the category or subcategory you want to fall under a different category.

3 Click Move.

4 Select the new category under which you want the previous category or subcategory to fall.

5 Click OK.

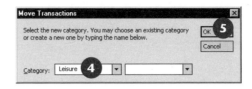

TIP

Restore standard categories.
If you want to restore the standard Money categories, or remove all unused categories, choose Options from the Tools menu, click the Categories tab, and then click the Restore Standard Categories or Remove Unused Categories buttons.

TIP

Get the details. *Click Go To Payee or Go To Category to display details about the selected payee or category.*

Delete a Category

1. Click More on the navigation bar, and choose Categories & Payees from the menu.

2. Select the category or subcategory you do not need.

3. Click Delete.

4. If you have existing transactions using this category, assign the transactions to a new category and then click OK.

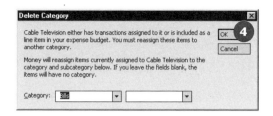

Rename a Payee

1. Click More on the navigation bar, and choose Categories & Payees from the menu.

2. Click Payees in the left pane.

3. Select the payee you want to rename.

4. Click Rename.

5. Enter a new name for the payee.

6. Click OK. If a payee already exists under the name you specify, Money asks whether you want the transactions rolled into the existing payee name. Click Yes.

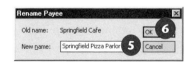

Entering Recurring Transactions

You can use Money's Payment Calendar to help keep track of recurring deposits, such as direct-deposit paychecks, and recurring bills, such as monthly utility bills and automatic mortgage or insurance payments. Money's Payment Reminder reminds you when these bills are due.

TIP

Preview recurring transactions. *Click Go To Calendar in the left pane to see which recurring transactions will be due during the month.*

Add a Recurring Payment

1. Click Bills on the navigation bar, and click New.

2. Click the Bill option button, and click Next.

3. Select the account from which you pay the bill.

4. Enter the date for the first payment.

5. Enter the name of the person or business you are paying.

6. Enter the amount of the payment.

7. Categorize the payment, and click Next.

8. Click the More Than Once option button, select how often the bill comes due from the Frequency field, and then click Next.

9. Select the payment method, and click Next.

10. Specify whether the payment is a constant amount or whether it varies, and click Next.

11. Specify whether or not you want Money to record the first payment, and click Finish.

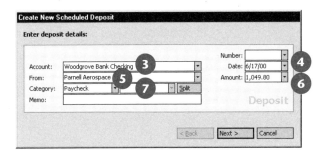

Add a Recurring Deposit

1. Click Bills on the navigation bar, and click New.

2. Click the Deposit option button, and click Next.

3. Select the account into which the deposit is made.

4. Enter the date for the first deposit.

5. Enter the name of the person or business paying you.

6. Enter the amount of the deposit.

7. Categorize the deposit, and click Next.

8. Click the More Than Once option button, select how often the deposit is made from the Frequency field, and click Next.

9. Select a deposit method, and click Next.

10. Specify whether the deposit amount is the same or whether it varies, and click Next.

11. Specify whether or not you want Money to record the first deposit, and click Finish.

Paying Your Bills

You can use the Bills area to quickly record in your account registers the payment of scheduled bills, the receipt of scheduled deposits, the occurrence of scheduled transfers, and the scheduled purchase of investments.

Record a Scheduled Transaction

1 Click Bills on the navigation bar.

2 Select the scheduled transaction or transactions you want to record.

3 Click Record. (The name of this button changes depending on the type and number of transactions selected.)

4 Use the form Money displays to edit the transaction and add any additional information (such as the check number you used to pay the bill).

5 Click Record. Money records the transaction in your register.

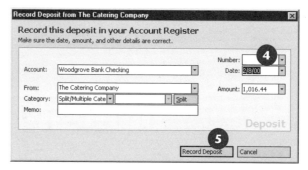

Fixing Errors

It's easy to fix mistakes you happen to make while entering checks, deposits, and account transfers in your account register. Deleting or voiding a transaction is even simpler.

TIP

Void instead of delete.
Money ignores voided checks when it calculates your account balance, and it doesn't include the checks in any reports. But it does keep a record of the voided checks, which is a very good practice.

Edit a Transaction

1. Go to the account register, and double-click the transaction you want to edit.

2. Click the field you want to edit.

3. Enter your correction, and click Enter.

Delete a Transaction

1. Right-click the transaction you want to delete.

2. Choose Delete from the shortcut menu.

3. Click Yes to delete the transaction.

Void a Check

1. Go to the account register.

2. Right-click the check you want to void.

3. Choose Mark As from the shortcut menu, and choose Void from the submenu.

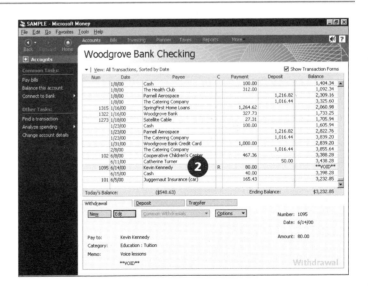

Finding Lost Transactions

Although Money can't help much in proving that you did indeed make that payment that got lost in the mail, it can give you a little peace of mind if you can't remember whether or when or how much you paid someone.

Search for Transactions

1. Choose Find And Replace from the Tools menu.

2. Select which types of accounts you want to search.

3. Enter the text or number you want to find.

4. Select which transaction fields you want to search.

5. Click Next. Money displays a list of the transactions it finds.

6. To view a transaction, double-click it in the list.

Use an Advanced Search.
Click the Advanced Search option button if a basic search does not return any transactions or if it returns too many transactions. An advanced search lets you broaden your search by selecting more than one possible entry in a field. It also lets you narrow your search by combining several search criteria.

Replace Information in Transactions

1 Click Replace after Money displays the list of transactions it finds.

2 Select the information you want to replace.

3 Specify what you want to substitute for the information.

4 Tell Money whether you want it to replace the information in all the listed transactions or in only those that you designate.

5 If you choose to select the transactions individually, put a check mark beside the ones you want to replace.

6 Click Next.

7 Click Finish.

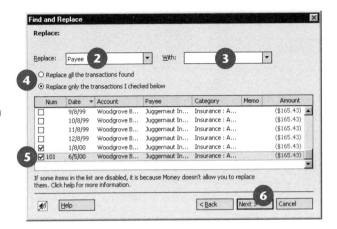

3

Reconciling Bank Accounts

Let's face it. One of the most tedious tasks in keeping a checking account is balancing, or *reconciling*, the account. Yet it's extremely important to do so. By comparing your records with the bank's, you can catch errors you've made in recording transactions and usually catch errors made by the bank as well. Only by regularly balancing an account can you protect yourself against problems such as forgery and embezzlement.

TIP

Record bank charges. *In Money's initial list of categories, there is a Bank Charges category for recording service charges.*

Reconcile a Bank Account

1. Display the account register for the bank account you want to reconcile.

2. Click Balance This Account in the left pane. Money displays an introductory Balance dialog box. Click Next.

3. In the next dialog box, enter the bank statement ending date in the Statement Date field.

4. Enter the bank statement opening, or starting, balance in the Starting Balance field.

5. Enter the bank statement closing, or ending, balance in the Ending Balance field.

6. If your bank statement shows a monthly service charge, use the Service Charge and Category fields to describe this expense.

7. If your bank statement shows any interest income, use the Interest Earned and Category fields to describe this income.

8. Click Next.

Balance Woodgrove Bank Checking

Enter the following information from your statement:

Statement date: 6/1/00

Starting balance: 40,458.08

Ending balance: 32,328.51

If applicable, also enter the following:

Service charge: 1.50
Category: Bank Charge / Service Char

Interest earned:
Category: Investment I / Interest

Next > Cancel

⑨ Mark the checks and deposits that have cleared the bank.

◆ Click in the C (for Cleared) column for all deposits that show on your bank statement. When you do, Money places Cs in this column to signal that these transactions have cleared the bank.

◆ Click in the C (for Cleared) column for all checks and withdrawals that show on your bank statement. When you do, Money places Cs in this column to signal that these transactions have cleared the bank.

⑩ When the difference between the cleared balance and the bank statement balance equals zero, click Next. Money congratulates you on balancing your account.

⑪ Click Finish. Money redisplays the account register in its usual format.

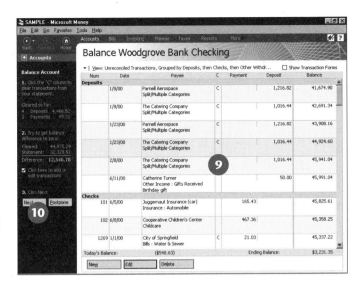

I Can't Get My Account to Balance

If, after you complete the step-by-step process described on the previous pages, the cleared balance still doesn't equal the statement balance, the problem probably lies in one of the following places:

◆ You made a mistake marking transactions as cleared.

◆ The register is missing one or more transactions.

◆ You or the bank recorded a transaction incorrectly.

If you find yourself in this situation, your best bet is first to be sure that your account register isn't missing a transaction. You can do this by checking that every transaction that appears on the bank statement also appears in the account register. I find, for example, that it's really easy to miss an automated teller machine (ATM) transaction or two. You can add a missing transaction directly in the Account Register window that shows when you're reconciling an account.

When you're sure that you've entered any missing transactions, verify that each transaction you recorded as "cleared" has really cleared. If you incorrectly marked an uncleared transaction as cleared, unmark it. If you accidentally left a cleared transaction marked as uncleared, by all means clear it.

Finally, compare the transaction amounts shown in your register with the transaction amounts shown on your bank statement. If you discover that you've entered one of your checks or deposits incorrectly, you can fix it by editing it in the list of unreconciled transactions. For example, you can change check or deposit information by clicking on the incorrect information and then editing or typing over the existing text or number.

Remember that in setting up your accounts, you need to begin with an accurate account balance, preferably a just-reconciled account balance. If you don't begin with an accurate balance, you might not be able to reconcile the account balance because your starting balance is wrong. In this case, there's not much you can do unless you want to go back to your old banking records and try to find the error or errors that made your starting account balance wrong. If you do find yourself in this situation, by the way, I suggest that you attempt to balance your bank account every month—and then give up once you can't go any further. (By clicking the Postpone button, Money saves your work and returns you to a regular view of the account register.)

This sounds lazy and perhaps crazy, but here's my logic. If you can't balance the account but the difference is the same every month—$41.35 in January, $41.35 in February, and $41.35 in March, for example—you'll know that the account won't balance because of errors you made at least as early as January. And in this case, I think it makes more sense to adjust the account balance so that your account does balance rather than waste any time looking for the error or errors that explain the mysterious $41.35. Money is, after all, supposed to make managing your finances less work, not more work.

To adjust the account balance, click Finish, even though Money still shows a difference between your records and the bank's. When Money displays the Balance Account dialog box, click the Automatically Adjust The Account Balance option button, use the Category field to categorize the adjustment, and click Next.

Two Notorious Bank Account Errors

Two types of bank account errors are notoriously difficult to catch, so let me tell you what they are and how you catch them.

♦ Transposing Numbers

For example, say you enter a check as $21.34 when it really should have been entered as $23.14. You've entered the correct digits, but in the wrong order. This error is tough to catch because as you look through your checks and deposits, you see the transaction, see that it has all the right digits, but fail to notice the transposed 1 and 3.

♦ Entering a Check as a Deposit or a Deposit as a Check

People make this error when they enter a transaction in the register but stick the amount in the wrong column. You can usually catch this error by marking your checks and other withdrawals as "cleared" in a batch and then marking your deposits as "cleared" in a batch.

Errors That Balancing Won't Catch

The main reason that you should balance bank accounts is to find errors you or the bank made in recording checks, deposits, and other transactions. But a reconciliation won't catch bookkeeping errors.

One such error is a transaction that you've forgotten to record in your account register and that hasn't yet cleared the bank. If the missing transaction is a check (and it most likely is a check, since you usually have more checks than deposits), you think you have more money in your checking account than you actually do. Unfortunately, the only way to avoid this error is to be diligent about recording your transactions.

Another type of error a reconciliation won't catch is a fictitious transaction you inadvertently recorded. Because the transaction is fictitious, it never shows up on a bank statement and is always listed as outstanding. Although the possibility of recording a fictitious transaction seems extreme, it can occur. You might, for example, record a weekly check to your daughter's piano teacher without actually printing the check.

Fictitious transactions have the opposite effect on your account balance than do uncleared transactions that you have forgotten to record: a fictitious check erroneously decreases the account balance, and a fictitious deposit erroneously increases the account balance. To prevent these errors, you simply need to be careful not to record transactions until they occur.

Closing Accounts

You probably don't close accounts very often, but if you do find yourself needing to close an account, you have two ways of telling Money that the account no longer exists. You can close the account so that you can still view its records and include its transactions in reports and charts, or you can delete the account and permanently remove all records of it.

Close an Account

1. Click Accounts on the navigation bar to display the Accounts Place.

2. Right-click the account you want to close.

3. Choose Account Is Closed from the shortcut menu.

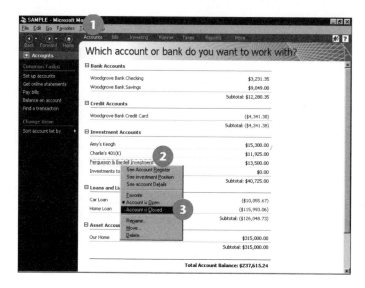

Delete an Account

1. Click Accounts on the navigation bar.

2. Right-click the account you want to delete.

3. Choose Delete from the shortcut menu.

4. If Money asks you to confirm the deletion, click Yes.

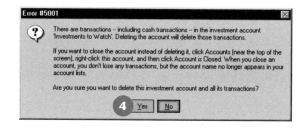

4

Keeping Track of Credit Cards

Almost every time I hear of someone in financial trouble, the person's credit cards seem to be one of the main culprits. Credit cards are by their very nature problematic. You're carrying around a little piece of plastic that can be used at whim to respond to the calls of sophisticated advertising. And once you've got that brand-new credit card and a high starting credit limit, there aren't really any obstacles to keep you from purchasing leather shoes you can't afford or expensive stereo gear you don't need. Then, after you fall behind and begin carrying a balance, breaking out of the credit card trap becomes more and more difficult.

Microsoft Money can help you deal with your credit cards by letting you track the money you're spending with a credit card and the balance you've accumulated. Keeping these records produces a couple of interesting benefits. The most obvious benefit is that you know where you're spending money and how much you owe on your credit card. There's also a more subtle benefit to using Money to track your credit card spending: if you're someone who finds it easy to spend freely with credit cards, the simple act of recording every credit card purchase tends to help you become more sensitive to the effects of saying, "Charge it."

Creating Credit Card Accounts

If you're already disciplined about how you use your credit card, you don't need to set up a credit card account. You can just record checks to the credit card company in the same way that you record any other check, splitting the transaction for each of the items you bought over the month. If, on the other hand, you do carry a balance on your credit card or you're not disciplined about your credit card spending, you should definitely set up a credit card account.

SEE ALSO

See "Using the Debt Reduction Planner" on pages 78–79 for information on how to plan your way out of credit card debt.

Set Up a Credit Card Account

1. Click Accounts on the navigation bar to display the Accounts Place.

2. Click Set Up Accounts in the left pane.

3. Click Add A New Account to start the New Account Wizard.

4. Enter the name of the bank or financial institution that issued your card, and click Next.

5. If you see your bank's name in the list that's provided, select it and then click Next.

6. Select Credit Card from the list, and click Next.

7. Enter a name for the account (or accept the default), and click Next.

8. If you know your account number, enter it and click Next.

9. The wizard asks how much you owe on your credit card. Enter the amount listed in the Previous Balance portion of your current credit card statement, and click Next.

Zero balance. *If you aren't carrying a balance from your previous credit card statement, you can save yourself a little time by entering your balance as zero. This way, you do not need to record the amount of your last payment.*

10 The wizard asks whether the card is a credit card or a charge card. Select the appropriate option, and click Next.

11 If you selected the credit card option, the wizard asks you about the card's interest rate. Enter the interest rate information, and click Next.

12 If your credit card has a credit limit, enter the limit and then click Next.

13 The wizard asks whether you want Money to AutoBalance your account each month. To indicate that you don't want to AutoBalance your account, click No and then click Next.

14 The wizard asks whether you want the credit card payments added to your list of recurring payments. If you do, check Yes and fill out the dialog box. Click Next.

15 Click the I Have No Other Accounts At This Institution option button, and click Next.

16 Click Finish.

Enter the payment amount you'll probably make here.

Specify the date by which you'll have to make your next payment on the credit card balance.

4

Recording Credit Card Purchases

To record a credit card transaction, display the account register of the credit card account. A credit card account register works the same way as a bank account register. To enter a credit card charge, use the transaction form at the bottom of the Account Register window.

SEE ALSO

See "Assigning Transactions to Multiple Categories" on page 29 for more information about splitting transactions.

TIP

Record interest when you reconcile. *Don't worry about recording interest and service charges. You record these amounts when you reconcile your credit card account.*

Record a Credit Card Purchase

1. Display the register of the credit card account.

2. Click the Charge tab. If the Charge tab is currently displayed, click New.

3. Enter the purchase date.

4. Enter the name of the person or business you paid.

5. Enter the amount of the purchase.

6. Click the down arrows in the Category fields to categorize the purchase, or click Split to split the transaction into more than one category.

7. Enter a note in the Memo field.

8. Click Enter to record the transaction.

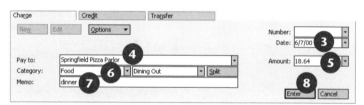

Recording Credit Card Credits

To record a credit card credit, such as you might receive when you return an item you bought with a credit card, you fill in the fields of the Credit tab the same way you fill in the fields of the Charge tab.

TIP

Record a credit as an expense. *Although it might seem strange to do so, you want to record the credit using an expense category, namely the same one you used when you recorded the original purchase. This way, the balance in the category will reflect this refund.*

Record a Credit Card Credit

1. Display the account register of the credit card account.

2. Click the Credit tab. If the Credit tab is currently displayed, click New.

3. Enter the credit date.

4. Enter the name of the person or business that refunded you.

5. Enter the amount of the credit.

6. Click the down arrows in the Category fields to categorize the credit.

7. Enter a note in the Memo field to help you remember why your account was credited: what exactly you returned or whether the business made a mistake when they charged your account.

8. Click Enter to record the transaction.

Reconciling Credit Card Accounts

Reconciling a credit card account works in exactly the same way as reconciling a bank account. Before you begin, you need your last credit card statement and preferably all your credit card receipts for the month.

TIP

Sobering statistics. *Some research suggests that people spend, on average, 23 percent more when they shop with a credit card than they do when they shop with cash. By the time you figure in the interest charges that often approach 20 percent annually, it's easy to pay close to 50 percent more for everything you charge on a credit card.*

Reconcile a Credit Card Account

1. Display the credit card account register.

2. Click Balance This Account in the left pane.

3. If this is your first time balancing this account, click Next to continue.

4. Enter the credit card statement ending date in the Statement Date field.

5. Enter the previous balance from your credit card statement in the Total Amount You Owed Last Month field.

6. Enter the new balance from the credit card statement closing balance in the Total Amount You Owe This Month field.

7. Use the Service Charge and Category fields to record service charges.

8. Use the Interest Charge and Category fields to record finance charges.

9. After you've completed the Balance Credit Card dialog box, click Next.

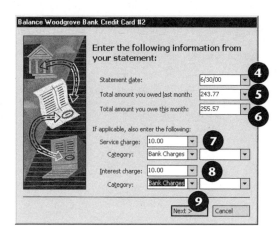

Balance Woodgrove Bank Credit Card #2

Enter the following information from your statement:

Statement date: 6/30/00

Total amount you owed last month: 243.77

Total amount you owe this month: 255.57

If applicable, also enter the following:

Service charge: 10.00 Category: Bank Charges

Interest charge: 10.00 Category: Bank Charges

Next > Cancel

Pay later. *If Money alerts you that you have a balance remaining but you want to postpone paying the credit card bill, you can click Pay Bill Later in the dialog box Money displays after you finish balancing the account. To later pay the bill, you record a transfer from your checking to the credit card account.*

⑩ Mark the purchases, credits, and payments that have cleared the account by clicking in the C (for Cleared) column. When you do, Money places Cs in this column to indicate that these transactions have cleared the bank.

⑪ When the difference between the cleared balance and the credit card statement balance equals zero, click Next.

⑫ Click Pay Bill Now to enter a transfer transaction for the credit card payment.

Recording Credit Card Payments

To record a credit card payment, you record the check that you use to pay the credit card bill in the appropriate bank account register. For example, to pay a credit card bill by writing a check on a bank account named "Woodgrove Bank Checking," you just write and record the check in the usual way. Then, rather than categorize the check, you can transfer the money to the credit card account.

TIP

Recording options. *As with any transfer transaction in Money, you can record a credit card payment either in the register of the account receiving the money (in this case the credit card account) or in the register of the account giving the money (in this case the bank account).*

Record a Credit Card Payment

1. Open either the credit card register or the register for the bank account you'll use to pay the credit card bill.

2. Click the Transfer tab. If the Transfer tab is currently displayed, click New.

3. Enter the check number.

4. Select the name of the bank account you're writing a check on.

5. Enter the transfer date.

6. Select the name of the credit card account you're paying.

7. Enter the amount of the credit card bill you're paying.

8. Enter the name of the credit card company.

9. Click Enter. Money records the credit card payment and recalculates the account balance for both accounts.

Tips for Getting Out of Credit Card Debt

Perhaps it's no surprise that with credit cards so easy to get, a fair number of people soon find themselves carrying credit balances they can ill-afford and each month only going deeper into debt. While for the most part, getting out from under this sort of burden simply requires belt-tightening and discipline, there are a handful of tried-and-true strategies for making this process easier:

♦ Make sure you've found the lowest-interest credit card available. The difference between a credit card with a high interest rate and one with a low interest rate can easily run 10 percent annually. And with even a relatively modest $2,000 balance on your credit cards, that means $200 a year in extra interest charges. You can check out credit card interest rates by calling local banks or visiting Internet web sites such as *www.bankrate.com.*

♦ Watch out for late payment fees and, of course, pay particular attention to the payment due dates. Merely paying a day or two late can add significantly to your credit card costs if you get hit with a 5 percent late payment penalty or a month's interest.

♦ Take a close look at any extra services or products the credit card issuer wants to sell you. Buying such financial products as life insurance or employment insurance from a credit card company is often not a good deal.

♦ As noted earlier in this section in a tip, simply not using a credit card typically saves you money. So that's something you'll want to consider. Note that because people typically spend 20 to 25 percent more with a credit card, even affinity credit cards—such as those that give you a rebate or airline frequent-flyer miles—don't really make good financial sense either.

♦ If you want to get out of credit card debt, start by paying off the card that charges the highest interest rate. Once that balance is paid, pay off the card with the next highest interest rate, and so on.

♦ Finally, although it may make sense to consolidate credit card debt into a tax-deductible home equity loan or into a low-interest personal loan, a word of warning is in order. In practice, these debt consolidation strategies often only let people get into more credit trouble. Some folks simply use the debt consolidation loan to go out and borrow additional money later.

4

Creating Reports and Charts

5

U sing Microsoft Money 2000 only for financial recordkeeping delivers some benefits. Money, for example, calculates account balances automatically and accurately. It prints checks for you. And after you begin using Money, you'll discover that reconciling a bank account takes only a couple of minutes.

But the biggest benefit of using Money isn't that it allows you to do all these things. The biggest benefit is that Money lets you sort and summarize the financial information you collect in many ways. By using Money's reports, for example, you can see how much you're really spending on housing, groceries, work expenses, and so forth. You can easily track and tally tax deductions. And you can compare your actual income and expenses with whatever amounts you budgeted.

You can work with reports in several ways using Money. You can produce on-screen reports and customize them to show exactly what you want to see. You can also save your favorite reports to see how your spending habits change, and you can print and export reports to easily take them with you and show them to others.

Producing Reports

The makers of Money realized the importance of being able to visualize your finances, which is why they made the reports feature so quick and easy to use. Within a matter of minutes, you can create a detailed report of some aspect of your finances and customize it to show exactly what you want.

Spending Habits

Produce an On-Screen Report

1 Click Reports on the navigation bar.

2 Click a category in the left pane to see a list of reports and charts that summarize a particular aspect of your finances.

3 Select a specific report or chart from the list.

4 Click Go To Report/Chart. Money produces the selected report or chart.

The Six Basic
Report Categories

CATEGORY	DESCRIPTION	PURPOSE
Spending Habits	Summarizes transactions by payee or category and compares actual income and spending with budgeted income and spending	Allows you to see how you earn and spend your money, where you earn and spend your money, and how your actual earnings and expenditures compare to your plans
What I Have	Summarizes account balances at a point in time or over a period of time	Allows you to estimate your net worth and to see the estimated value of your assets and liabilities
What I Owe	Summarizes liability account balances and post-dated payment transactions	Allows you to gauge the magnitude of your debts and to plan repayment strategies
Investments	Summarizes investment account and transaction information	Allows you to assess the profitability of your investments and to perform year-end investment tax planning
Taxes	Summarizes tax-related transactions	Shows you what taxable income and tax deductions you'll report on your year-end tax return and allows you to perform year-end tax planning
Monthly Reports (Money 2000 Deluxe)	Summarizes your spending habits, net worth, investment performance, potential problems, tax information and Advisor FYI tips for the month	Allows you to view several aspects of your financial situation during any given month and compare the information with other months

5

Working with Reports

After you create a report, you might want to turn that report into a chart so you can easily see the information. With the click of a button, you can create a chart from a report and then customize the chart to your liking. When you have your report or chart just the way you want it, you can save it so that you don't have to recreate it the next time.

TIP

3D distorts data. *You probably want to keep the Show In 3D check box clear because three-dimensional charts frequently distort data.*

Create a Chart

1 Display or create the report from which you want to make a chart.

2 Click a Chart toolbar button.

3 Click Customize.

4 Use the Chart tab in the Customize Report dialog box to customize the chart.

◆ Click Bar to create a bar chart; then use the Stacked check box to tell Money whether you want your bars displayed side by side or in a single column.

◆ Click Line to create a line chart.

◆ Click Pie; then use the Pie Labels option buttons to tell Money how to label the pie chart.

5 Click Apply to preview the chart.

6 Click OK to return to the Chart window.

Use this field to specify where you want to display a legend.

Open a favorite report. *To open a report or chart you have added to the My Favorites list, click My Favorites in the left pane and double-click the report or chart in the My Favorites list.*

Add a Report or Chart to the My Favorites List

1 Display or create the report or chart you want to add to your My Favorites list.

2 Choose Add To Favorites from the Favorites menu.

3 Enter a name for your customized report in the Report Name box.

4 Click OK.

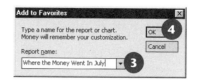

Producing Month-End or Year-End Reports

Money is capable of producing many different reports and charts. As a result, deciding which reports to produce can be a bit overwhelming. Fortunately, you can apply some good rules of thumb in this area. You should print out an Account Transactions report at the end of every month and file it with your bank statement and canceled checks. And you should print a Tax-Related Transaction report at the end of each year and store it with a copy of your tax return.

TIP

Printed reports can save you. *If you forget to back up your Money data, you can re-enter all the transactions from your Account Transactions reports to rebuild your financial records.*

Create an Account Transactions Report

1. Click Spending Habits in the left pane.

2. Select Account Transactions from the list.

3. Click the down arrow in the Accounts field, and select an account from the list.

4. Click the down arrow in the Date Range field, and select Previous Month from the list.

5. Click Go To Report/Chart.

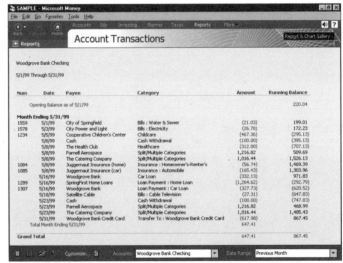

SEE ALSO

See Section 6, "Personal Financial Planning," for information on how Money 2000 Deluxe makes it easier to plan your income taxes and prepare your income tax returns.

TIP

Export transactions to a tax program. *To create a Tax-Related Transactions report to export to a tax preparation program, click Taxes in the left pane, select Tax Software Report from the list, and then click Go To Report/Chart.*

Create a Tax-Related Transactions Report

1. Click Taxes in the left pane.

2. Select Tax-Related Transactions from the list.

3. Click the down arrow in the Date Range field, and select Previous Year from the list.

4. Click Go To Report/Chart.

Customizing Reports and Charts

Since Money offers more than two dozen reports and charts, you can usually find one that answers the questions you have. Nonetheless, Money gives you a rich set of customization options that you can use to change the appearance of reports and charts.

TIP

Some reports have different options. *Which tabs and available options appear in the Customize Report dialog box depends on the report. Different reports have different customization options.*

Change the Layout of a Chart

1 Display the report or chart or select it in the Report & Chart Gallery.

2 Click Customize.

3 Click the Rows & Columns tab.

4 Use the Rows & Columns tab's boxes and buttons to specify several layout options, including:

◆ What you want the rows and columns of the report to list

◆ How you want subtotals calculated

◆ How you want transactions sorted

◆ Which transaction fields you want included in the report

◆ Whether you want the chart to show a running balance

◆ What level of detail you want the report to show

5 Click OK.

Filter the Information Included in a Report or Chart

1. Display the report or chart or select it in the Report & Chart Gallery.

2. Use the field or fields available at the bottom of the window to customize the most common options.

3. Click Customize.

4. Use the Customize Report dialog box's Date, Account, Category, Payee, Text, Details, and Amount tabs to filter the information you want included in the report or chart.

5. If you're currently viewing the report or chart, click Apply to see your changes.

6. Click OK to close the dialog box and display the report or chart.

Use this tab to specify the type, status, or check or number of transactions you want included in the report or chart.

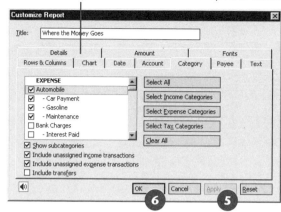

Reset a Report or Chart to the Default Settings

1. Select the report or chart you customized from the Report & Chart Gallery.

2. Click Reset.

3. Click Yes.

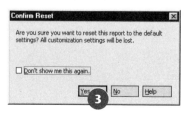

Formatting Reports

Once you have your report created and customized to show the information you want, you can also format it so it's pleasing to the eye and easy to read.

TIP

Undo customizations. *To undo all customization and formatting changes, click Reset.*

Change the Column Widths

1. Select or display the report.

2. Click Customize.

3. Click the Fonts tab.

4. Select one of the Report Column Widths options.

5. Click OK.

Customizations don't affect data. *You can't hurt your data by summarizing it in reports or by depicting it in charts, so feel free to experiment with customizing your reports.*

Change the Font Style and Point Size

1. Select or display the report.

2. Click Customize.

3. Click the Fonts tab.

4. Select a font from the Font list box.

5. Select a font size from the Size list box.

6. Click OK.

Printing Reports

Although on-screen reports are great, especially because you can create and manipulate them so quickly and easily, you may also want printed copies of your reports so you can take them with you and show them to others—to your accountant, for instance.

Set Up Your Printer

1 Choose Print Setup from the File menu.

2 Choose Report And Chart Setup from the submenu.

3 Select an Orientation option to specify whether Money should print pages in portrait or landscape orientation.

4 Click Options to display the printer's Properties dialog box, which you can use to change the paper tray, the print quality, and so forth. Click OK to return to the Report And Chart Setup dialog box.

5 Click OK.

Print charts too. *To print a chart, display the chart and then choose Print from the File menu and then specify the print settings using the Print Chart dialog box.*

Print a Report

1 Display the report you want to print.

2 Choose Print from the File menu.

3 Select Print Range options to specify which part of your report you want to print.

4 Specify the number of copies to print in the Copies box.

5 Click OK to print the report.

How Long to Keep Records

People throw around many different rules for retaining canceled checks, bank statements, copies of old tax returns, and other financial records. I suggest that you keep everything for seven years after you file a tax return. If you filed 1991's tax return in April 1992, keep all your 1991 tax return records until April 1999.

The reason you should hang on to your records for so long is that the Internal Revenue Service can examine returns as old as seven years. The IRS can't go back any further than that, except in a handful of very special cases. So as long as you keep everything together for at least seven years, you'll almost certainly be okay. (The "very special cases" have to do with businesses with net operating loss carry-forwards and taxpayers with foreign tax credits. If you don't know what these are, they probably don't apply to you. But consult a tax advisor if you're not sure.) If you're ever audited, you can use Money to print a summary of your deductions, and you can verify this report with the canceled checks.

You should save some documents for much longer than seven years. When I say to retain records for seven years, I'm referring only to financial records. Hang on to insurance records permanently, for example, because it's possible in some circumstances to file a claim against a policy from years and years ago. You should also permanently retain many legal documents. (Consult an attorney for information on this.)

Exporting Reports

Exporting means to move a report to another application. You export reports so that you can manipulate the data in some way or use the data in another document. For example, you might export a report so that you can analyze it in a spreadsheet application such as Microsoft Excel. Or you might want to include a report in a word processing document.

TIP

Exported report file format.
When you export a report, Money creates something called a tab-delimited text file. *Tab-delimited text files are easy for spreadsheet applications to import and open, and they can also be imported and opened by most word processing applications.*

TIP

Import into other programs.
To import the tab-delimited text file into another application, just open it from the other application. (You may need to indicate that the exported file uses the .txt extension.)

Export a Report

1. Display the report you want to export.

2. Right-click the report, and choose Export from the shortcut menu.

3. Click the down arrow in the Save In drop-down list box, and specify where Money should save the exported report.

4. Enter a filename in the File Name box.

5. Click OK.

6

Personal Financial Planning

Personal financial planning might sound sophisticated, but it's really not. When you boil it down, personal financial planning covers three common-sense activities:

◆ Arranging your day-to-day financial affairs so you can spend more time enjoying life rather than worrying about how you're going to pay the bills

◆ Choosing and then plotting a course toward major, long-term financial goals, such as buying a house, sending kids to college, or retiring

◆ Creating a financial safety net so that a personal tragedy or unexpected expense doesn't mean financial disaster

Fortunately, Microsoft Money 2000 Deluxe provides the Planning Center tools to successfully address just these planning issues. This section discusses these important tools, describing in detail how you work with the most useful of the tools and providing sidebar discussions of related financial strategies.

Using the Lifetime Planner

Perhaps the most powerful and useful personal financial planning feature available within Money is the Lifetime Planner. The Lifetime Planner allows you to construct a detailed, written financial plan that summarizes your current financial condition—and plots a path to future financial success.

Run the Lifetime Planner

1. Click Planner on the navigation bar.

2. Click Planner in the left pane, and then choose Lifetime Planner from the menu.

3. Optionally, click the Watch video hyperlink to display a short video that describes the Lifetime Planner.

4. Click Next to begin construction of your personal financial plan.

5. Follow the on-screen instructions when you're prompted by Money. For example, when Money displays the About You window, enter your name, birth date, and the age at which you plan to retire. If appropriate, enter your spouse's name, birth date, and the age at which he or she plans to retire. Then add any dependents you have or plan to have in the future.

Average annual returns. *The Lifetime Planner asks what investment return you expect. You may be interested in knowing, therefore, that over long periods of time common stocks have averaged about 9 to 10 percent, while long-term bonds have averaged about 5 to 6 percent, and small company stocks have averaged about 12 percent. These are gross return numbers. Your return would be reduced by any investment expenses you pay.*

Income tax rates. *The Lifetime Planner asks you about the income tax and inflation rates you expect. Experiment with a variety of tax and inflation rates to see how sensitive your plans are to changes in these important variables.*

Navigate within the wizard. *You can move backward to a previous dialog box by clicking the Previous button. You can then move forward, predictably, by clicking the Next button. The Previous and Next buttons appear in the upper right corner of the window.*

6 To continue through the Lifetime Planner, click Next and answer the questions that Money asks.

7 When you finish the planning process, but before you click Finish, choose Print from the File menu to print a paper copy of your plan.

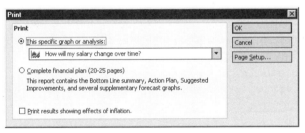

6

Tips for Retirement Planning

Before you determine how much you need to save to reach your retirement income goal, you need to set a goal for yourself and also see how much you can save in employer pension plans.

Set a Retirement Income Goal

People throw around all sorts of rules of thumb about this figure. In my case, for example, I figure that I want to live pretty much the same way when I'm retired as I do right now. Of course, when I'm retired, I won't have to make my mortgage payment—my mortgage will have long since been paid by then. And I won't have to pay Social Security or Medicare taxes—you only pay Social Security and Medicare taxes on earned income, not on unearned income, which is what retirement income is. I also won't have the work expenses, such as work clothes and commuting costs, that I now have. So if I take my current income and subtract my mortgage payment, my Social Security and Medicare taxes, and my work expenses, I get a retirement income number that lets me live the same way I do now. Note that if you live in a big house but plan on moving to a small condominium, for example, you can reduce your retirement income goal even more.

The basic calculations you make for determining your retirement income are as follows:

1 Look at your current income.

2 Adjust it for expenses you won't have once you're retired.

The caution I'll give, however, is that you don't want to be too optimistic about reducing your expenses. It's pretty safe to assume that you won't have a mortgage payment when you retire at age 62 if, for example, your mortgage will be paid off by age 59. And while no one knows how the tax laws will change between now and the time you retire, I also think it's pretty safe to assume that your retirement income won't be subject to Social Security and Medicare taxes. But I'd be cautious about assuming you can, for example, tighten up your living expenses, or get by with just one car if you and your spouse now drive two.

Consider Employer Pension Plans

As you consider strategies for saving money for retirement, I should say that there is one wildcard here—your employer's pension plan. I think you can probably rely on your employer's pension plan. And it just may be that your employer's pension plan will provide you with all the retirement income you need. But you need to be careful.

One factor that you need to worry about a little is whether your retirement income benefits depend on your continued employment. Let me explain.

One kind of retirement plan, called a *defined benefit plan,* pays you retirement income based on your salary in the final year or years you worked. With this type of plan, for example, you might receive a pension benefit of $32,000 if you work 40 years for a big company and make $40,000 in your final year.

A defined benefit plan, such as the one I just described, can be a great deal for employees. In fact, if your employer has a plan like this and you can be sure of some day receiving the benefits, you probably don't need to save a dime for retirement. No kidding.

But there's a problem with defined benefit plans if you work for a number of different employers instead of working for one employer for many years. This is true even if all the employers have the same "2 percent for every year you work" benefit formula.

The problem is that the figure on which your retirement income is based—your final year's or years' salary—will be very low for all but your last employer or two. Inflation causes this, of course. And so does the fact that people tend to make less in their early working years.

To see how this works, suppose that you work some place for 40 years, that you're making $40,000 a year in your final years, and that you receive a retirement benefit equal to 2 percent of your final salary for every year you worked. In this case, for your first 10 years of work you would get $8,000 of retirement income (10 × 2% ×

$40,000). This would be true even though you were probably making far less at that time.

Now consider the case of your neighbor. Let's say she had four different jobs over her working years. Let's say her first job, the one she worked during the first 10 years of her career, paid less because it was a less demanding job. And, of course, 30 years of inflation have passed since she left that job. So maybe her salary at the 10-year marker was $7,000. In this case, for her first 10 years of work she'll get a retirement benefit from that employer of $1,400 (10 × 2% × $40,000).

Do you see the scary part of this? You, for your first 10 years of work, accumulate $8,000 of retirement income, but your neighbor, for her first 10 years of work, accumulates $1,400. Your neighbor's situation is even worse if she switched jobs more frequently—say, every couple of years or so. If that was the case, because of the way that pension benefit calculations work, it's possible for your neighbor to have *no* retirement benefits at all for her first 10 years of work.

What I've just described is, in a nutshell, the problem with defined benefit retirement programs. They can be wonderful deals for long-term employees, but for people who switch jobs frequently, they don't amount to such a good deal. Please note, too, that even if you have the best of intentions about staying some place for your entire career, you can't really be sure you'll do this. Companies downsize. Industries decline. What you want to do with your life may change.

6

Planning for College

College costs vary widely by region, but generally speaking, four years at a public university cost almost $40,000. Four years at a private university cost about $80,000, and four years at a select private university cost close to $120,000. Despite the high costs of college, however, your kids can go. As long as you have an idea about the kind of college your child will attend, you can come up with a pretty good estimate of how much you need to save. The Lifetime Planner includes a dialog box you can use to see how much college costs for just about any four-year college or university.

Investing College Savings

When you start saving money for your child's college expenses, you'll need to decide whose name to put on the savings account. You can hold the savings in your name, in which case you'll be taxed on the investment income the savings produce, or you can give the savings to your child, in which case your child will be taxed. In general, you pay less income tax by putting money in your child's name. If the child is 14 years old or younger, the first $700 or so of investment income is tax-free, and the next $700 is taxed at the lowest marginal income tax rate. If the child is 15 years old or older, the first $4,250 of income is tax-free (this might include both investment income and earned income if the child now has a job), and roughly the next $25,000 of income is taxed at the lowest marginal rate.

The one awkward thing about putting the money in a child's name is that the money really does become the child's. You can't borrow it temporarily—even if you have a good reason to do so. And when children reach the age of majority, either 18 or 21, they can spend the money on anything they want.

The other tricky thing about deciding whether to put the savings in the child's or in the parent's name has to do with current financial aid regulations. These regulations assume that basically all of a child's savings are available for college but that only a portion of his or her parent's savings are available.

Despite the risks, I recommend using a custodial account to save money for college expenses if you're going to initiate a long-term, substantial college savings program. You trust your kids, and you yourself are subject to income taxes. If you're not going to initiate a long-term, substantial savings program, or your kids have some of the troubles that many kids do, or your income tax burden is very light, I'd say go ahead and keep the money in your name.

Where Should You Invest College Savings Money?

As long as you start early—preferably while your child is still in diapers and definitely not long after your child starts grade school—I think it makes sense to invest college savings money in the stock market. Go for something that's well diversified and inexpensive. (A no-load stock index fund based on the Standard & Poor's 500 Index is what I've got my kids' college money in.)

If you figure on the stock market delivering its historical average of 10 percent and you subtract about 0.2 percent for expenses, you can figure on your college savings money earning about 9.8 percent. That's pretty good.

Then, at some point in the future, you'll want to begin moving money from the stock market into something very safe. Some financial writers advocate moving money from stocks to short-term bonds or certificates of deposit four to five years before you need it. This means moving a child's college freshman year money from the stock market to bonds at roughly the time the child is a high school freshman. Move more money into safer

investments in each of the next three years to provide for the child's sophomore, junior, and senior years of college.

If you don't feel comfortable with the stock market as a savings vehicle, you might want to consider another gambit. What you might do is save money for your kid's college by prepaying your mortgage. In other words, rather than save, say, $50 a month and invest this sum in the stock market, you could instead just add this amount to your monthly mortgage payment. Your goal in following a plan such as this would be to pay off your mortgage completely by the time your child enters college. What would then happen is that just as your college bills start, you suddenly wouldn't have a mortgage. You could then redirect your mortgage payment toward your child's college expenses. Note that most families could send at least one child to a public university following this sort of plan. And, with a bit of effort, many families could even pay to send two children to public university by following this plan.

I don't recommend using your retirement accounts for college savings. While it's true that retirement accounts aren't generally counted in college financial-aid calculations, and while it's also true that you get a significant tax benefit in some cases by doing this, I think you need to reserve your retirement accounts for something far more important than your kids' college bills. Specifically, I suggest you reserve your retirement accounts for your own retirement.

6

What to Do If You Can't Afford College

Even if you can't afford a dime for your kids' college education, your kids can still figure out a way to go to college and even go on to graduate and professional school. They will have to be a bit more flexible. They may need to be a bit more creative. But with some work and planning—and perhaps, more important, the desire—any kid can go to college. It's more important to offer emotional support and encouragement than cold, hard cash.

For this reason, don't worry if you can only save, say, 50 or 75 percent of what your calculations show as necessary. If you can just start saving money regularly—especially if you start early—you can make good progress.

Let me also mention that I have several friends who successfully and solely paid their ways through both college and graduate and professional school. They all describe the experience as positive and a source of real pride. But enough said. Let's look at the down-and-dirty mechanics of saving serious money.

Basically, saving for college comes down to reducing either of the variables in the following formula:

Annual College Costs × Years of College = Total College Costs

If you start brainstorming, you can quickly come up with a lot of good ideas for reducing the costs of college.

In the lists that follow, I describe the best ways I know of to reduce annual college costs as well as the number of years it takes to complete college.

Here are ways to reduce the cost of going to college:

◆ Attend a community college for the first two years rather than a public university. This saves $8,000 over the first two years.

◆ Attend an equivalent public university instead of a private university. This can save tens of thousands of dollars over four years.

◆ Live at home rather than in student housing, and attend a college as a commuter student. Your savings with this tactic are about $1,200 a year (the net of commuting costs).

◆ Get a part-time student job, such as a dormitory resident assistant. This saves $3,000 (usually paid as free room and board).

◆ Do a one-quarter work-for-credit study that pays a real salary. This saves $3,000 in earnings during the quarter.

◆ Work at the college as a full-time employee. Many colleges will then allow you to take a part-time class load for free or for a nominal fee.

Here are ways to reduce the amount of time spent in college:

- Take Advanced Placement (AP) classes in high school. (If your child's high school doesn't offer Advanced Placement classes, you can also arrange for College Level Examination Program, or CLEP, examinations.) Many high schools offer half a dozen AP classes, and some offer twice that number.

- Take a transferable community college class during the summer breaks. You can shave off one quarter or even a semester this way.

- Take an extra class a year. Or take an extra class each quarter or semester if you can take the extra class for free.

I know that some of the tricks and techniques included in the two preceding lists aren't exactly appealing. But if someone has to choose between going to college on a shoestring budget or not going at all, college on a shoestring budget is the better choice, by far.

Applying for Financial Aid

To determine whether a student is eligible for financial aid, you need to fill out the Free Application for Federal Student Aid, or FAFSA. The information you provide on this statement determines the amount the government and colleges expect you to contribute to your child's educational expenses. The financial aid formulas expect you to live at the poverty line—about $15,000 for a family of four—and then contribute between 10 and 20 percent of the income you make in excess of the poverty line to your child's college expenses. Your child is expected to earn and contribute about $1,000 per year and pay whatever savings he or she has toward the expense of college. Whatever amount is left over after deducting these amounts determines the amount of financial aid for which the student is eligible.

Financial aid comes in three types: grants, loans, and work-study programs. Grants are "free money" that doesn't need to be repaid, but are available to only the neediest of students. College loans are much more prevalent, and loans are available in several forms. Some loans are given to parents, while others are given to students. Some loans are through a bank, while others come directly from the federal government. Some loans are need-based and do not require you to pay interest on the loan until the student graduates from college, while other loans are unsubsidized and not based on need. Last, work-study programs allow qualified students to help pay for their college costs by working for an approved employer, often on campus. To find out more about financial aid programs available at the college your child plans on attending, inquire at the college's financial aid office.

6

Using the Debt Reduction Planner

Another useful personal financial planning feature available within Money 2000 Deluxe is the Debt Reduction Planner. The Debt Reduction Planner allows you to map out a detailed plan for repaying all your debts—credit card, consumer loans (like those for a car or boat), and even a mortgage.

TRY THIS

Navigate within the wizard.
You can move backward to a previous dialog box by clicking the Previous button. You can then move forward, predictably, by clicking the Next button. The Previous and Next buttons appear in the upper right corner of the window.

Run the Debt Reduction Planner

① Click Planner on the navigation bar.

② Click Planner in the left pane, and then choose Debt Reduction Planner from the menu.

③ Click Next.

④ Review the loan and credit card accounts listed in the Debt Plan.

⑤ If you see an account listed in the Debt Plan that shouldn't be there, click the account and then click Move Out Of Plan.

⑥ If you see an account that isn't included in the Debt Plan but should be, click the account and then click Move Into Plan. Specify the size of payment you want to make in the Amount To Be Paid field.

⑦ If you notice a loan or credit card account missing from the list in the Debt Plan, click New Account. Then run the wizard that Money starts to describe the debt and set up an account.

⑧ Click Next to define your payment plan.

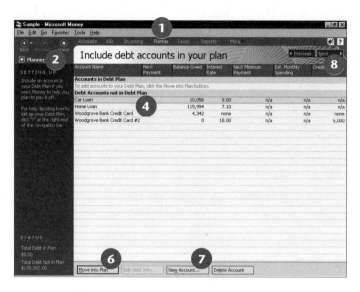

Decide when to repay. *As a general rule, you want to repay debts before whatever you bought with the borrowed money wears out. With this rule, then, it's fine to borrow money to buy a house using a 30-year mortgage because a house will last much longer than 30 years. But it's generally inappropriate to borrow money to buy items that wear out quickly (such as clothing) or that you'll consume immediately (such as food) unless you plan to immediately repay the debt.*

9 If you want to define your payment plan by making a specified payment, select the What I Want To Pay Each Month option button, and then move the slider to set the payment amount. Note that you can also set a one-time payment amount.

10 If you want to define your payment plan by getting out of debt by a specified date, select the Date I Want To Be Out Of Debt option button, and then move the slider to set the deadline date.

11 Click Next. Money displays a line chart that graphically depicts your debt reduction plan.

12 Click Next. Then, optionally, schedule the payments required for your debt reduction plan.

13 Click Finish.

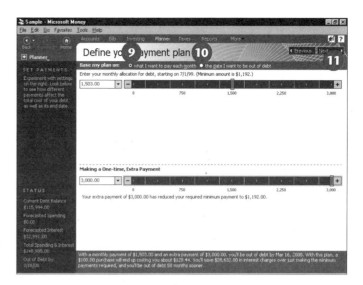

Using the Budget Planner

The best way to arrange your day-to-day financial affairs is to summarize how you spend your income and then create guidelines for your spending. Most people call this "budgeting." Once you've decided how to budget your income and expenses, recording that budget with Money is simple. All you do is describe how much you'll earn or spend in each income or expense category.

TRY THIS

Create a report. *Produce one of Money's Spending Habit reports to use as a guideline in your budgeting. Section 5, "Creating Reports and Charts," describes how you produce reports.*

Run the Budget Planner

1. Click Planner on the navigation bar.

2. Click Planner in the left pane, and then choose Budget Planner from the menu.

3. Click Next.

4. Follow the on-screen instructions, paying particular attention to the contents of the Money Help window. When Money displays the Income tab, for example, use it to identify which categories of income you'll receive and the deposits you'll record.

5. Continue to move through the Long-Term Savings, Occasional Expense Fund, Debt, and Expenses tabs. Follow the on-screen instructions for completing the budget-planning tasks associated with each tab.

To add a new category of income not shown, click the Add Category button.

TIP

Build a budget. *If you have Money 2000 Standard, click Budget on the navigation bar to build a simple budget.*

TIP

Navigate within the wizard. *You can move backward to a previous dialog box by clicking the Previous button. You can then move forward, predictably, by clicking the Next button. The Previous and Next buttons appear in the upper right corner of the window.*

⑥ When you reach the Monthly Summary tab, review the monthly budget information for accuracy and reasonableness, and then click Next.

⑦ When you reach the Yearly Summary tab, again, review the annual budget information for accuracy and reasonableness, and then click Next.

⑧ Review the Forecast tab for a detailed graphic view of your budget.

6

Six Ways to Stretch Your Budget Dollars

Take Aim at Your Biggest Expenses

If you've been working with Money for any length of time, produce a Spending Habit report and look at your three largest spending categories. (These spending categories probably constitute most of your spending.) Next, sit down with your family and brainstorm about ways to reduce these expenses.

What you're doing here is only rational. It's much easier to carve out $25 a month of savings in a category in which you're spending $500 a month than it is in a category in which you're spending $50 a month. To save $25 in a $500-a-month expense, you need to figure out how to shave off only 5 percent. To save $25 in a $50-a-month expense, you need to figure out how to chop off 50 percent.

Even if your three biggest spending categories are your housing, car, and grocery bills, if you want to find extra money, you're more likely to succeed by looking wherever you're currently spending the most money. Moving from a three-bedroom apartment to a two-bedroom apartment, for example, will save probably 10 percent or more on your housing expenses. So will moving into a smaller house.

If a housing change is too traumatic, consider driving a less expensive, more gas-efficient car or taking the bus. Try to arrange a car pool. If your family uses two cars, consider getting rid of one.

Live Healthier

Here's a strange coincidence. If you make healthy lifestyle choices, you usually save money. Quit smoking, for example, and you easily add $30 or $40 to your monthly cash flow. If you're a heavy smoker, you could add even more. Moderate your alcohol consumption or quit drinking alcohol, and you can save just as much money each month. And there are the less obvious healthy choices: drinking less coffee, eating less meat, cutting down on sweets, walking or biking rather than driving.

To find out where you're spending money on bad habits, keep a record of where you spend each and every dollar for a few days. Then look at the list. The following table shows a sample list along with the annual cost of the habit.

ITEM	COST	POSSIBLE YEARLY SAVINGS
Specialty morning coffee	$1.75	$437.50 (if every working day of year)
Cookie after lunch	$0.90	$225.00 (if every working day of year)
Cigarettes	$3.00	$1,095.00 (if pack-a-day smoker)
Six-pack after work	$5.00	$520.00 (if two six-packs a week)

Think Green

If you're environmentally conscious, you can also save money—probably quite a lot. Don't drive if you can walk. Turn your thermostat down a few degrees. Shorten your showers. Turn lights and appliances off when you're not using them. By participating more fully in recycling and composting you can almost eliminate garbage bills. Take good care of your car and make the necessary repairs, and you may be able to drive it for 200,000 miles and keep it out of the junkyard for an extra 10 years. If you don't have prejudices about secondhand goods, you can purchase just about anything—clothing, furniture, cars—at great savings. By becoming less of a consumer, you save money and are kind to Mother Earth at the same time.

Stop Using Your Credit Card

Research suggests that people spend about 23 percent more on purchases when they shop with a credit card. If you then pay 15 percent or 20 percent interest on the money you've borrowed with your credit card, you end up paying almost 50 percent more for everything.

Given the propensity to spend more with credit cards, one thing you can probably do to save money is stop using your credit card. If you're skeptical about this gambit, by the way, just try it for a week or two. You may find yourself buying less expensive lunches and not purchasing certain items altogether.

Find One Expense That Wastes Money

Without knowing the specifics of your situation, I suspect you have one or two expenses that, if you didn't make them, would not affect your life at all. For example, do you subscribe to magazines that you never get around to reading? Do you pay to store a boat, an RV, an antique car, or a motorcycle 12 months of the year and only bring it out to enjoy once or twice a year? Consider pulling the plug on the expense. While there probably is some emotional reason for making the expenditure, cutting these kinds of expenses doesn't affect your standard of living.

Find One Expense That You're Willing to Compromise

Another tactic that makes sense is to compromise some area of your spending. Decide right now that you're going to find an area where you will make do with less by living frugally or by making small sacrifices. Then go out and pick the one expenditure in your budget that means the very least to you. Maybe it's athletic club dues or the premium cable television stations. This sounds silly, but it usually works. It's often difficult to decide to save, say, $1.00 a day, but it's easier to decide to save a dollar a day by not stopping for coffee on the way to work any more.

6

Using the Home Worksheet

The Home Worksheet lets you estimate how much you can afford to pay for a house, based on both your income and your existing debt, and calculating what size home or what size mortgage payment you can afford.

Estimate Home Affordability

1. Click More on the navigation bar, and then choose House Center from the menu.

2. Click the How Much Home Can I Afford hyperlink.

3. Click the Information tab.

4. Use the Calculate field to indicate what you want to calculate: the cash you'll spend, the monthly payment you'll make, the purchase price, or some combination of these variables.

5. Use the Information tab's fields to describe the home purchase in as much detail as you can. Note that you don't have to fill a field you've told Money to calculate.

Enter your income.

Enter your total monthly debt service payments.

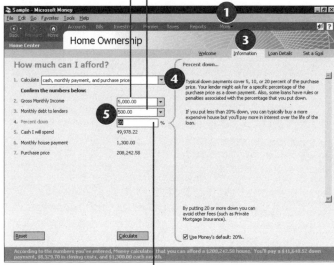

Enter the total cash you will pay for the down payment and closing costs.

Use the Home Center. *The Home Center includes links to other tasks and resources useful for home buyers. For example, click the Find A Home hyperlink to search home listings online using the MSN HomeAdvisor Finders.*

⑥ Click the Loan Details tab.

⑦ Use the Loan Details tab's fields to describe the mortgage you'll use. Note that Money supplies its best guesses for most of the variables.

⑧ Click the Set A Goal tab to see a snapshot summary of your home affordability calculations.

Enter the annual property taxes.

Enter the closing costs you'll pay as a percentage of the purchase price.

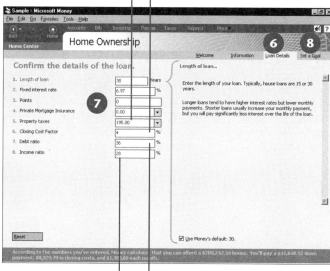

Enter the lender's maximum allowable housing-costs-to-income ratio.

Enter the lender's maximum allowable debt-to-income ratio.

6

Using MSN's MoneyCentral

The Microsoft Network's (MSN's) MoneyCentral web site provides a rich set of tools—articles and calculator wizards—that you can use to make better personal financial decisions. There isn't room in this book to describe in detail all of MoneyCentral's tools—and, in fact, MoneyCentral grows and gets better all the time. Nevertheless, I do want to whet your appetite for the useful tools and information you'll find at MoneyCentral.

Reviewing the MoneyCentral Articles

MoneyCentral provides numerous general articles on personal financial planning topics. To access these articles, visit the MoneyCentral web site at *http://www.moneycentral.msn.com* and then click the hyperlink that corresponds to a category of personal financial-planning articles. (To easily visit the MoneyCentral web site, enter the web site address in your browser's Address box or choose Microsoft On The Web from the Help menu and Microsoft Money Home Page from the submenu, and then click the MSN MoneyCentral hyperlink.) For example, if you want to see a list of articles about family finances, click the Family Finance hyperlink. Then click the article you want to read.

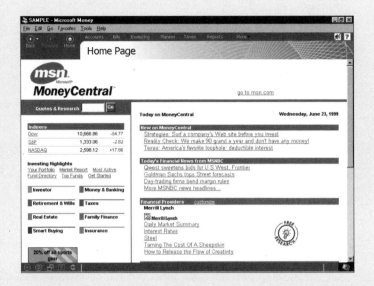

When MoneyCentral displays the article, you can read it online using the Page Up and Page Down keys to scroll through the text. As you read MoneyCentral articles online, watch for hyperlinks that point to other interesting Internet resources. You can also choose Print from the File menu to print a paper copy of the article.

Reviewing the MoneyCentral Calculators

MoneyCentral provides almost two dozen calculators, including Savings, Debt Consolidation, Debt Evaluation, Retirement Expense, Retirement Income, Life Expectancy, Roth IRA, Deduction Finder, Loan Comparison, Buy vs. Rent, Second Income, Time Value, and Tuition Savings.

The MoneyCentral calculators all use self-descriptive names. The Tuition Savings Calculator, for example, estimates how much you'll need to save for a child's college costs and also how much college might cost in the future. The Debt Evaluation Calculator calculates what percentage of your income you spend on debt payments and then assesses the reasonableness of this ratio in light of a prospective lender's underwriting standards.

The MoneyCentral calculators are easy to use. They each start a simple wizard that helps you make a useful calculation—such as how much you should save for a child's future college costs. The following figure shows the first window used by the Tuition Savings Calculator.

To use one of the calculator wizards, simply fill in the blanks and click buttons. Most calculators require you to complete several steps. Click Next to move ahead, or return to a previous step—suppose you need to make a change—by clicking Previous.

Using the Loan Planner Worksheet

The Loan Planner Worksheet lets you analyze and compare loan alternatives. To use this worksheet, describe the loan or loans you're considering in precise terms. The worksheet then calculates the loan payments and total costs.

Analyze a Loan

1 Click More on the navigation bar, and then choose House Center from the menu.

2 Click the Calculate The Costs Of A Loan Or Compare 2 Loans hyperlink.

3 Click the Initial Costs tab.

4 Use the Initial Costs tab's fields to describe the loan or loans you're considering.

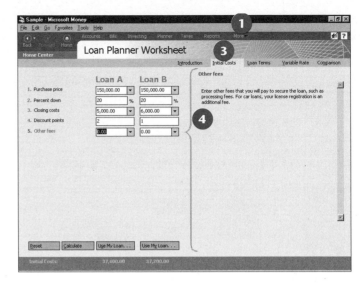

Adjustable rate mortgages.
If you want to analyze an adjustable rate, or variable rate, mortgage, click the Loan Worksheet's Variable Rate tab. Then use its fields to describe the variable rate loan you're considering.

5 Click the Loan Terms tab.

6 Use the I Want Money To Calculate field to indicate what you want to calculate: the length of the loan, the principal and interest, the loan amount, the starting interest rate, or the balloon payment amount.

7 Use the other fields to describe the loan or loans in greater detail. Note that you don't have to provide the loan variable you want Money to calculate.

8 Click Calculate to calculate the variable you didn't supply.

9 Click the Comparison tab to display an analysis of the loan or loans you're considering.

Using the Home Inventory Worksheet

The Home Inventory worksheet lets you build a list of all your personal property. You might do this if you want to build a record of valuable assets you've insured.

Inventory Your Household Items

1 Click More on the navigation bar, and then choose House Center from the menu.

2 Click the Keep Track Of My Possessions hyperlink.

3 Click New.

4 Click the down arrow in the Asset Type field, and select an asset group description from the list.

5 Enter a brief description of the item in the Description field.

6 Use the Location field to indicate where you've stored the item or where you use it.

7 Use the Current Value, Replacement Value, and Purchase Price fields to describe what you originally paid for the item—and what you estimate it would cost to replace the item. You can also use the Purchase Date and Purchased At fields for further documentation.

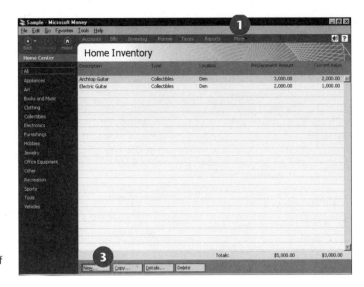

8 Optionally, provide additional information about the item, such as the model, make, and serial number.

9 Click Enter. Money adds the item to the Home Inventory.

10 Repeat steps 4 through 10 for each of the items you want to add to the Home Inventory.

11 Choose Print from the File menu to print a paper copy of the Home Inventory worksheet.

6

Using the Tax Estimator Worksheet

The Tax Estimator worksheet lets you estimate what you'll pay in income taxes for the year. To use this worksheet, describe your filing status, income, and deductions. This easy-to-use tool, by the way, can be a financial lifesaver if your income and deductions make it impossible for you to estimate your income taxes.

TIP

Estimate capital gains. *To estimate your capital gains taxes, click Taxes on the navigation bar, click Calculate Capital Gains Taxes, and then use the worksheet that Money displays to indicate which investments you'll sell.*

Estimate Income Tax Expense

1. Click Taxes on the navigation bar.

2. Click the Estimate Your Taxes hyperlink.

3. Click Overview in the left pane. Then use the Tax Estimator worksheet fields to describe your filing status, number of dependents, other deductions, spouse deduction, the year for which you're estimating taxes, and the estimated taxes you've already paid.

4. Click Income in the left pane. Then use the Tax Estimator worksheet fields to describe your income, including your wages and salary, interest and dividends, capital gains, alimony you receive, unemployment, and other income items.

Access Internet tax advice.
MoneyCentral provides lots of good tax-planning information. To access this help, click Taxes on the navigation bar and then click Learn About Current Tax Strategies.

⑤ Click Adjustments in the left pane. Then use the Tax Estimator worksheet fields to describe any adjustments for adjusted gross income, including any contributions to tax-deferred retirement accounts (such as an Individual Retirement Account), self-employment taxes and medical insurance deductions, alimony you pay, unreimbursed moving expenses, and other adjustments.

⑥ Click Deductions in the left pane. Then use the Tax Estimator worksheet fields to describe any itemized deductions you're allowed, including medical and dental expenses, real estate and property taxes, deductible investment interest, mortgage interest, charitable contributions, casualty and theft losses, and miscellaneous deductions.

⑦ To see your estimated income tax expenses, click See Results.

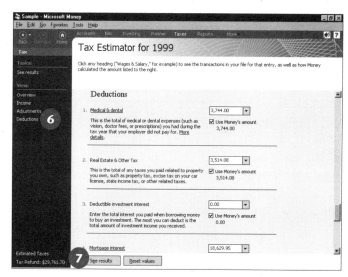

The Four Best Ways to Save Money on Taxes

Take Every Deduction You're Entitled To

I continually run into people who don't take all the deductions they're entitled to. Some of them think they increase their risk of being audited by taking too many deductions. Others think maybe they're being a little unpatriotic by taking too many deductions. But not taking every deduction you're entitled to is a big mistake. The U.S. Congress writes the tax laws with the assumption that taxpayers will take every deduction to which they're entitled.

If you routinely give away clothing your kids have outgrown to the local thrift shop, for example, be sure to collect a receipt, assign a fair value, and then take the amount as a charitable donation deduction. If you're spending money on night school so that you can acquire new skills and get a better job, take the amount as an employee business expense deduction.

Bunch Your Deductions

Perhaps the best way to save money on income taxes without giving up anything in return is to bunch your deductions so that you take the standard deduction in some years and itemize deductions in other years. This effectively increases your deductions. Let me explain. Let's say you're married and that you routinely have about $8,000 a year in itemized deductions.

Furthermore, just to make the math simple, let's also assume that you can take a $7,000 standard deduction. In any given year, then, it makes sense to take the $8,000 a year in itemized deductions because that reduces your income tax bill. But if you pay some deductions early and some deductions late, you can actually increase the total deductions you're taking over time. Why? Because (and this is the trick) in the years when your itemized deductions fall below the standard deduction amount, you can take the standard deduction. Let me show you how this works over a four-year time frame.

Let's say that your plan is to use the standard $7,000 deduction in years 1 and 3 and itemized deductions in years 2 and 4. In this case, you want to pay as many of your deductions as you can in years 2 and 4. The table below shows an example of what your itemized deductions could be in years 1, 2, 3, and 4 if you did this kind of juggling.

ITEMIZED DEDUCTION	YEAR 1	YEAR 2	YEAR 3	YEAR 4
Mortgage interest	$5,500	$6,500	$5,000	$7,000
Real estate taxes	0	$3,000	0	$3,000
Charitable donations	0	$2,000	0	$2,000
Total	$5,500	$11,500	$5,000	$12,000

Because you get to choose whether to itemize or use the standard deduction, you itemize in years 2 and 4, but you take the standard deduction in years 1 and 3. If you itemize in each of the four years, you'll have $32,000 of deductions (four years times $8,000 a year). If you simply take the standard deduction, you'll have $28,000 of deductions (four years times $7,000). But by bunching your deductions and then flip-flopping between the standard deduction and itemized deductions, you can deduct $37,500.

Exploit Retirement Savings Options

Tax-deferred investment options such as 401(k)s, 403(b)s, IRAs, SEP/IRAs, and Keoghs are such good deals that I can't promote them enough. If you're saving for retirement (and you should be), these tax-deferred investment options are absolutely the best way to go.

Don't Use Nondeductible Consumer Credit

Another very powerful tax-savings gambit is to convert nondeductible consumer credit interest on items such as car loans, credit cards, personal lines of credit, and so forth to deductible mortgage or home equity loan interest. To do this, you need to be a homeowner, of course. But assuming you are, you could take out, say, a $25,000 second mortgage home equity loan and use the proceeds to pay off your car loan, all your credit cards, a student loan you're still paying on, and any other debts you might have.

If you swap $25,000 of consumer credit that charges 10 percent interest with a $25,000 home equity loan that charges 10 percent, for example, you still pay $2,500 a year in interest, but you can use the $2,500 of home equity loan interest as a deduction. If your marginal, or highest, income tax rate is 28 percent, you save about $700 a year. If the home equity loan's interest rate happens to be lower than the average interest rate you're paying on all the consumer credit you replace—and it probably is—you save even more money.

Despite the substantial savings available, I caution you regarding this particular gambit, especially if you're someone who likes to use a credit card. Sure, if you do one of these home equity loan things and use the proceeds to pay off your consumer credit debt, it may save on taxes. But you won't be in any better shape if you go out and start charging up your credit cards again. More than a few people take out a home equity loan and then find themselves with both a $25,000 home equity loan and a bunch of new credit card debts.

Let me mention one other problem: you could end up stretching out the repayment of your debt. Swapping a deductible home equity loan for a nondeductible car loan sounds like a good idea. And it really may save on taxes. But you might not get ahead if your car loan has 3 years of payments left and your new home equity loan lets you make payments over the next 10 years.

6

Exporting Money Data to a Tax Program

If you use Money to record all your income and expense and you also use a tax preparation program to prepare your federal and state income tax returns, you may want to export your Money data directly to the tax preparation program. This can save you time, and it may reduce errors.

Export to a Tax Preparation Program

1. Click Taxes on the navigation bar.

2. Click the Save Tax Data As A TXF File For Use With Other Tax Software hyperlink.

3. Indicate which tax year's data you want to export by selecting the year from the Review Taxes For box. Then click Continue.

4. When Money displays a list of the types of tax information it can export, indicate which types of information you want to export. Then click Continue.

5. Print out the report of your tax information by choosing Print from the File menu.

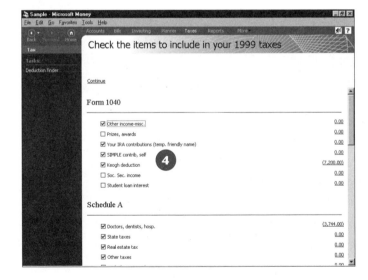

Export options. *You can use the TXF file that Money creates to export tax information to almost any tax preparation program.*

TaxSaver time saver. *If you're a TaxSaver user, you only have to complete step 5. After completing step 5, simply start the TaxSaver program.*

6 Click the Export Your Tax Information As A Data File You Can Use With any Tax Software Program hyperlink.

7 Name the TXF file by entering a filename in the File Name box. Then click OK.

8 Start the tax preparation program, and follow its instructions for importing a TXF file.

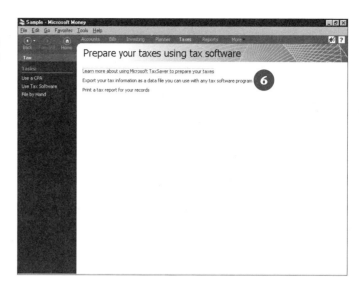

Prepare your taxes using tax software

Learn more about using Microsoft TaxSaver to prepare your taxes
Export your tax information as a data file you can use with any tax software program 6
Print a tax report for your records

6

7

Tracking Assets and Liabilities

Microsoft Money 2000's strength lies in keeping records of financial assets such as bank accounts, money-market funds, and investments, as well as in tracking liabilities such as mortgages and credit cards. But besides tracking these sorts of assets and liabilities, you can also use Money to track whatever else you own. And using Money for all detailed and thorough financial record-keeping can deliver enormous benefits.

If you're a homeowner, for example, you can keep a record of the improvements you've made to your home—and that can save on taxes later. By monitoring the money you borrow and what that money costs you (in interest), you can do a much better job of planning and managing your day-to-day financial affairs. You'll also be able to calculate your net worth more accurately—and that can lead to better personal financial-planning decisions.

Creating Asset Accounts

To track your net worth, you set up asset accounts for each major asset you own: your house, the car or cars you drive, and any other large, valuable items. You may also want to set up a catchall account for tracking the items that perhaps aren't especially valuable individually but collectively add up to a significant value, things such as baseball cards or silverware.

TIP

Current value or original cost. *If you're setting up an asset account for a house, enter the house's original cost.*

TRY THIS

Appreciation and depreciation categories. *If you're recording an increase in value, don't use an expense category to categorize the transaction. Instead, create a category to describe depreciation and appreciation of assets by entering Market Adjustment in the Category field.*

Create an Asset Account

1 Click Accounts on the navigation bar to display the Accounts place.

2 Click Set Up Accounts in the left pane.

3 Click the Add A New Account hyperlink.

4 Click the Not Held At A Bank, Brokerage, Or Other Financial Institution option button, and click Next.

5 Select Asset from the list, and click Next.

6 Enter a name and date of purchase for the asset account, and click Next.

7 Enter the current value of the asset or its original cost, and click Next.

8 Specify whether a loan account is associated with the asset account by clicking the Yes or No option button, and click Next.

9 If you indicated that a loan account is associated with the asset account, click the down arrow in the Loan Account field and select the loan account from the list.

10 Click Finish.

Tracking Assets

Once you've set up an asset account, it isn't difficult to keep a record of the asset and track the changes in its value. As with recording a check in a bank account register, you use the transaction forms at the bottom of the Account Register window to track changes to the value of an asset.

Track an Asset

1. Display the register for the asset account.

2. Click the Decrease or Increase tab, depending on whether you're describing a negative or positive change in the asset's value.

3. Enter the date of the change.

4. Optionally, enter the name of the person or business you paid if you made improvements on the asset.

5. Enter the amount of the change.

6. Click the down arrow in the Category field, and select an expense category.

7. Optionally, enter a description of the change in the Memo field.

8. Click Enter to record the increase or decrease and recalculate the asset account's balance.

Tips for Tracking Assets

Asset accounts work very much like bank accounts, and the mechanics of keeping track of an asset with Money are straightforward. Asset record-keeping, however, can be a little tricky.

Your Home

A home is usually a person's single largest asset. If you own a home and have decided to track your net worth with Money, you'll want to set up a home, or personal residence, account and use it to track the value of your home.

The historical appreciation of real estate makes it tempting to track the fair market value of a home. However, it may make more sense to track the original cost of the home as well as the cost of any home improvements. Although current income regulations exempt the first $250,000 of capital gain on the sale of a primary residence ($500,000 if married), homeowners who hold the same property for long periods of time and then enjoy steady appreciation can still exceed these limits. For example, a single taxpayer who purchases a $150,000 home and then experiences 4 percent inflation will have unrealized capital gains of roughly $330,000 thirty years in the future!

Even if you think that you won't own a home for the long time necessary to accumulate large, unrealized capital gains, you may still want to keep a record of your home's cost as well as the cost of improvements you make to it. There's no harm in doing so, the work is extremely minimal, and you might someday save a lot of money if tax laws change again.

To keep a record of a home's cost and the cost of improvements, you first set up an asset account named something like "Home" or "Residence." (I described how to do this on page 100.) In this account, you record as transactions the original cost of the home as well as associated purchase costs, such as escrow fees and title insurance. In the future, whenever you spend money to improve your home, you transfer the money from your checking account to the asset account set up for your home.

What qualifies as an improvement? Anything that adds value to a home or to its useful life. For example, adding a swimming pool, finishing the basement, and landscaping the site all qualify as improvements. However, maintenance costs such as those for painting the exterior or interior, repairing a leaky roof, or fixing faulty electrical wiring don't qualify as improvements.

The only problem to this approach is that your financial records don't show the value of your home—only the total of its cost and any improvements. If you want to also show the home's value, you can add a trans-action to your asset register that adjusts the account's total to the home's market value. Just be sure to delete this transaction before you calculate the capital gain stemming from the sale of the home.

Cars, Boats, and Other Personal Property

Cars, boats, and other valuable personal property can usually be handled nicely with individual accounts. In general, you don't need to make a lot of adjustments to the value of these assets. And you probably won't make improvements that increase their value, anyway. So you may just want to periodically—say, at the end of each year—update the account balances so that the asset's ending balance approximates its fair market value.

Asset Lists for Property and Casualty Insurance

It's not a bad idea to maintain records of the assets you've insured with a property insurance policy. The reason for this is probably clear: if disaster strikes, a list of the insured items can make claim reports and collections easier and more complete.

If you have Money 2000 Deluxe, you can create this list using the Home Inventory worksheet, which is described on pages 90–91. If you don't have Money 2000 Deluxe, you can set up another asset account called something like "Personal Property" and carefully list all assets you've insured. The more information on your list, the better. If possible, include information such as model numbers and original costs. Remember that you can use the Split Transaction dialog box to store additional data. Another great way to create an asset list for insured personal property (such as the contents of your home) is to walk through your house with a video camera and record what's in each room. You can also provide narrative descriptions of the items you're filming as you shoot the video.

One other point. Your asset list won't do much good if your computer and all your backup disks or your videotape are lost in a fire or flood (or whatever casualty destroys or damages the property you've insured). For this reason, you should probably keep an up-to-date copy of your asset list in a secure place, such as a safe-deposit box.

Setting Up Loan Accounts

Tracking a loan with Money is very easy, especially if you're already familiar and comfortable with tracking a bank account and you know how to transfer money between accounts. To begin tracking a loan, all you need to do is find the paperwork that describes the loan and its current balance (probably the last monthly statement) and then use the New Account Wizard to set up an account for the loan.

TIP

Adjustable rate mortgages. *If you're describing an adjustable rate mortgage, enter the date of the next adjustment and the length of the period between adjustments.*

Create a Loan Account

1. Click Accounts on the navigation bar, and click Set Up Accounts in the left pane.

2. Click the Add A New Account hyperlink.

3. Enter or select the name of the financial institution to whom you'll make your payments, and click Next. Verify the name of the financial institution, and click Next.

4. Select Loan from the list, and click Next three times.

5. Click the Borrowing Money option button, and click Next.

6. Enter the loan name and the lender, and click Next.

7. Specify whether the loan is a fixed or adjustable rate mortgage, and click Next.

8. Specify whether you have already made payments on the loan, and click Next.

9. Enter the date when you made the first loan payment, and click Next twice.

10. Select a payment frequency from the drop-down list box, and click Next.

⑪ Select the option that corresponds to your interest-calculation method, and click Next.

⑫ Enter four of the five loan calculation variables in the dialog boxes Money provides. Click Next.

⑬ Click OK to accept the loan variable Money calculated for you, and click Next twice.

⑭ Specify which expense category you want to use to track the loan expense, and click Next.

⑮ Specify whether the loan is a house loan, and click Next.

⑯ Specify whether the interest on this loan is tax-deductible, and click Next twice.

⑰ If you have any other charges or fees you have to pay on the loan, such as property taxes or insurance premiums, click Other Fees and enter the fees in the dialog box.

⑱ Tell Money whether you want to be reminded of the loan payment, and click Next twice.

⑲ Specify whether an asset account is associated with the loan. If so, select the asset account from the list box. Click Finish.

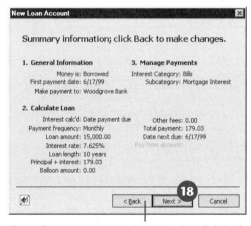

If you discover you've made a mistake, click Back to backtrack your way through the New Loan Account Wizard's dialog boxes.

Setting Up Liability Accounts

If your loan won't be amortized, you set up a liability account instead of a loan account. Setting up a liability account works very much like setting up other accounts.

TIP

Loan amortization.
Amortization means that your loan payments include not only the interest but also the principal. Over time, as the principal payments reduce the loan's balance, more and more of each payment goes toward reducing the loan's balance. Conventional home mortgages and most car loans are amortizing loans.

Create a Liability Account

1. Click Accounts on the navigation bar to display the Accounts Place.

2. Click Set Up Accounts in the left pane.

3. Click the Add A New Account hyperlink.

4. Enter the name of the financial institution to whom you'll make your payments, and click Next.

5. Verify the name of the financial institution, and click Next.

6. Select Liability from the list, and click Next.

7. Enter a name for the liability account, and click Next.

8. Enter the ending liability balance (the amount you still owe), and click Next.

9. Click the I Have No Other Accounts At This Institution option button, and click Next.

10. Click Finish.

Entering Liability Account Payments

If you set up a liability account, you record in your checking account any check that pays interest or principal for the liability in the usual way.

TIP

Record loan account payments. *You enter loan account payments in the same way you enter liability account payments. The only difference is that Money remembers the principal and interest breakdowns you provided when you set up the loan account, so it enters most of the payment information for you.*

TIP

Record principal. *If you're recording a payment of principal only, you can use the Transfer tab.*

Record a Liability Account Payment

1. Display the register for the checking account from which you want to write the liability account payment.

2. Click the Withdrawal tab. If the Withdrawal tab is currently displayed, click New.

3. Enter the check number.

4. Enter the check date.

5. Enter the lender's name in the Pay To field.

6. Enter the payment amount.

7. Describe the payment in the Category fields, or click Split to record a check that pays both interest and principal.

8. If you're splitting the transaction, use the Transaction With Multiple Categories dialog box to categorize each part of the transaction.

9. Click Enter to record the payment.

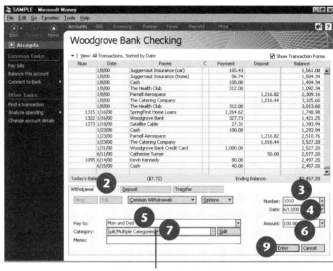

If you record a check that pays only interest, categorize it as an interest expense.

Describe the interest part of the payment on the first line, and categorize it as an interest expense.

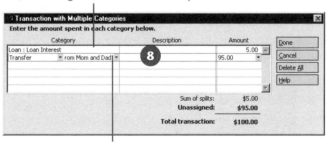

Describe the principal part of the payment on the second line by recording a transfer to the liability account.

Fixing Loan Account Balance Errors

Even though Money calculates the interest and principal portions of the loan payments you make, Money's calculations might still be wrong. This is especially true if the interest calculation is based on the date the payment is received by the lender. In this case, a delay in the mail of just a few days can create a difference in Money's calculation of the interest and the lender's calculation of the interest. Fortunately, it's easy to fix these kinds of errors.

Correct a Loan Account Balance

1. Display the register for the loan account.

2. Compare the ending balance for the account with whatever shows on the loan statement.

3. If your register balance varies from the loan statement, click Update Amount Owed in the left pane.

4. Enter the ending balance from your monthly statement.

5. Enter the ending date from your monthly statement.

6. If any fees are not accounted for in your records, categorize the fees in the Category For Adjustment field.

7. If you want to manually adjust the loan account balance so that it matches the statement, click OK to adjust the balance.

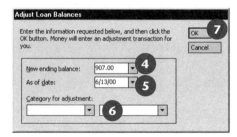

TIP

Balance every month. *It's a good idea to balance your loan account each time you get a monthly statement.*

SEE ALSO

See "I Can't Get My Account to Balance" on pages 40–41 for information about what to do when you can't get an account to balance.

⑧ If you want to balance the loan account in the same way that you balance checking accounts, click Balance. When you do, Money starts the Balance Account Wizard, which you can use to balance the loan account in the same way that you balance a bank account.

7

When to Repay and Refinance Mortgages

To determine whether it makes sense to repay a mortgage (or any other debt) early, you need to compare the interest rate the loan charges with the interest rate or investment return that some other investment pays. The rule is simple: your loan's interest rate needs to exceed the investment's interest rate or investment return in order for early loan repayment to make sense. If your mortgage charges 8 percent interest but you can buy a bond that pays 10 percent, for example, you shouldn't "invest" your money by repaying your mortgage early. You end up with more money by investing in the 10 percent bonds.

As a general rule, too, I should tell you that except in unusual situations (when your mortgage interest rate is in double-digits, for example), early mortgage repayment is probably not all that great a deal. If you can stick more money in your employer's 401(k) or 403(b) plan or in a tax-deductible individual retirement account (IRA), the 401(k), 403(b), or IRA always beats early mortgage repayment. In fact, it's not even a contest.

What About Your Other Debt?

While you get truly awesome interest savings when you look at the effect of repaying a long-term loan like a mortgage early, it's really a better deal to get out from under your credit card debt and other consumer credit debt.

Interest on consumer credit, such as credit cards and car loans, isn't tax-deductible. So a credit card that charges, say, 16 percent, really does cost 16 percent, whereas an 8 percent mortgage doesn't really cost 8 percent. Depending on your income tax situation, you get a tax deduction that effectively lowers your 8 percent mortgage to something between 5 percent and 7 percent. In effect, by paying off a credit card that charges a 16 percent interest rate, you make a 16 percent profit on your investment. (Your investment is paying off the credit card early.) If you pay off a mortgage that charges an effective, after-income-taxes-are-figured, interest rate of 5 percent, you make a 5 percent profit on your investment.

There's one other point that I should make about early repayment of debts. The idea is sound, but it doesn't really pay off if you go out and replace your old debt with new debt. That might sound funny, but let me explain. Paying off your mortgage early sounds like a great deal—and it is a great deal, really. But if you pay your mortgage off early and then, because you don't have mortgage payments, go out and purchase a new, larger, more expensive home, you're not really getting ahead. And if you get that credit card paid off early, but then you go out and fill your closet with a dazzling new wardrobe, you're not getting ahead that way either.

If you're paying a mortgage, it's easy to wonder whether you should refinance when interest rates drop. The logic seems straightforward enough: replace an expensive mortgage with a cheap mortgage and save money. Unfortunately, figuring out whether you'll actually save by refinancing a mortgage is very difficult.

Refinancing in a Nutshell

The trick to refinancing a mortgage is to make sure that you pay less for the new mortgage—taking into account both the interest charges and any refinancing costs—than you pay for your existing mortgage. To see if you pay less, you need to consider the interest rate and the refinancing costs, of course, but you also need to think about how long you'll be paying interest.

Fortunately, you can use MoneyCentral's Loan Comparison Calculator, which is briefly described on page 87, to perform this analysis. You use the Loan Comparison Calculator generally as described in its online instructions, but with several minor twists.

When you describe your existing mortgage as the first mortgage (Mortgage A), don't worry about the loan fees and payments you've already made. For your existing mortgage, then, there aren't discount points, loan service fees, or closing costs. And for your existing mortgage, the loan balance and the scheduled loan length equal what is left for you to pay, not what you originally had to pay.

Does all that make sense? Think about it for a minute and it should. When you consider refinancing a loan, you basically compare two loans: your existing loan, for which you'll pay no extra discount points, no loan service fees, and no closing costs, and a new mortgage, for which you'll pay all these extra charges.

The Complicating Factor

Unfortunately, there's also a complicating factor when it comes to mortgage refinancing. If you want to refinance as a way to save money over the long haul, you shouldn't do it as a way to stretch out your payments. In other words, you're very unlikely to save money by replacing an existing mortgage that has 15 years of payments left with a new, refinanced mortgage that requires 30 years of payments. Even if the new mortgage's interest rate is much lower, you'll be borrowing the money for a lot longer with the new mortgage.

8

Investing in Stocks, Bonds, and Mutual Funds

Microsoft Money provides wonderful tools for investment record-keeping. If you're an investor, you've probably already considered whether and how to use Money to make investment record-keeping easier and less time-consuming.

In general, there are two good reasons for using Money to track your investments.

◆ Your investments affect your income taxes. If you have investments that aren't tax deferred, you need to track your investments with Money so you know the taxable investment income that your investments produce and so you know about any capital gains or losses that occur (which will be taxable) when you sell an investment.

◆ You want to use Money's investment reports to assess the performance of your investments because you can't get annual investment return information somewhere else. By using Money's investment performance report, you can calculate the rate of return for the investments you're holding.

To get started with investment record-keeping, set up investment accounts and describe your current investment portfolio. After you complete these preliminary tasks, you can use Money for day-to-day financial record-keeping.

Setting Up Investment Accounts

To track your investments, set up at least one investment account. The general rule is to set up one investment account for each brokerage account statement you receive.

TIP

Tax-deferred accounts. *If you're investing money in tax-deferred accounts (and this is a smart thing to do), you won't have any taxable investment income because you won't have any capital gains or losses from your investments, so you don't really need to use Money to track this account.*

Set Up an Investment Account

1. Click Accounts on the navigation bar.

2. Click Set Up Accounts in the left pane.

3. Click Add A New Account. Money starts the New Account Wizard.

4. Optionally, enter the name of the financial institution associated with the account, and click Next.

5. If you see your bank name in the list provided, select it, and then click Next.

6. Select Investment from the list of accounts, and click Next.

7. Enter a name for the investment account, and indicate the account's currency.

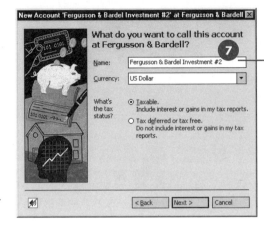

If you're setting up one investment account for each monthly statement, you may want to provide the name of the mutual-fund management company or stock brokerage company.

8. Specify whether the account is taxable or tax deferred, and click Next.

9. Click the No I'll Do This Later option button to answer the question about whether you want to describe each of the investments in your account. Then click Next.

10. Enter the estimated value of the investments in the account. Or, optionally, just leave this blank if you don't know or aren't sure.

11. If the investment has an associated cash account, enter the cash account's ending balance from your last monthly statement, and click Next.

12. If you entered a financial institution name in step 3, click the I Have No Other Accounts At This Institution option button.

13. Click Finish.

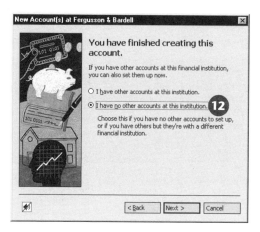

Describing Your Portfolio

Once you've set up your investment account, you're ready to describe the investments in your portfolio. You need to create these individual investments so you can work with them later.

TIP

Record the lot price. *It's usually a good idea to enter each investment lot separately if you purchased different lots at different prices because this technique often allows you to save on capital gains taxes. If you don't want to go to this much work or your investments aren't subject to capital gains taxes, however, you can just enter all the lots together as one big lot and use the average price you paid.*

Describe Your Current Portfolio

1. Display the investment account's register by clicking Investment Transactions in the left pane after opening the Account Summary.

2. Click New.

3. Enter the date you first purchased the investment.

4. Enter a name for the investment.

5. Click Enter to display the Create New Investment dialog box.

6. Select the option that most closely describes the investment you're adding, and click Next.

7. Use the fields that Money provides to describe the investment in more detail, and click Finish.

8. Click the down arrow in the Activity field, and select Buy from the list.

9 Enter the number of shares you own.

10 Enter the cost per unit you paid.

11 Enter any sales commission you paid.

12 Review the contents of the Total field, and edit the value if necessary.

13 Delete the account name shown in the Transfer From field. You don't want to reduce the cash balance for this transaction if it's an old investment purchase.

14 Click Enter to record the investment.

15 When Money asks how you want to treat the cash portion of this transaction, indicate that you don't want to track the cash.

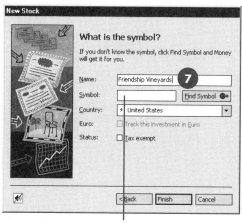

If you plan to use Money's Online Quotes feature, enter the security symbol.

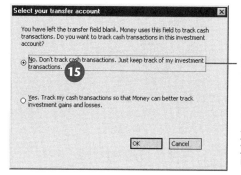

You don't track the cash for old transactions because their cash effects have already been included into the cash balance you provided when you set up the investment account.

The Portfolio Window

Once you've set up your investment accounts, described your investments, and updated their prices, you can use the Portfolio window to monitor your investments. To display the Portfolio window, click Investing on the navigation bar.

Click one of the tabs to view your investments in a different way or get financial markets news.

Click See A Different View to display a menu that lists the various ways you can view your investments.

This window lists your investment accounts and individual investments.

Right-click an investment, and then choose the Go To Investment Activities command from the shortcut menu to display the account details for that investment.

Using Online Quotes

The explosion in online investing means that you can get free, only-slightly-time-delayed online quotes from a variety of Internet sites as long as your computer connects to the Internet. Money recognizes this fact and provides you with the ability to retrieve individual quotes and also quotes for each of the investments in your portfolio.

TIP

Time-delayed quotes. *In general, the online quotes you receive for free are somewhat time-delayed. For example, a quote might be 20 minutes out-of-date.*

Retrieve an Individual Quote

1. Click Investing on the navigation bar.

2. Under Get A Quick Quote, enter the stock symbol in the text box.

3. Click Go.

When Money retrieves an individual quote, it also retrieves a variety of other useful information about the security.

Updating Prices

After you've described all the investments in your portfolio, you can tell Money to collect current price information (if you have an Internet connection) or even enter current price information manually. You may want to do this so your investment records reflect current market values.

TRY THIS

Real-time news reporting. *MSN's MoneyCentral web site also provides access to breaking news stories about the individual stocks in your portfolio. If MoneyCentral's web site identifies a news story related to one of your investments while it's updating prices, it places a "news" hyperlink next to the security name in the Investment Center. To read the story, click the hyperlink.*

Automatically Update the Prices in Your Portfolio

1. Display the Portfolio window.

2. Click Update Prices in the left pane.

3. Choose Update Price Automatically from the menu. Money will retrieve updated prices every time you connect to the Internet.

Update Price Online...
Update Price Manually...

✔ Update Price Automatically

When you choose Update Price Online, you tell Money to immediately connect to the Internet using your usual Internet connection and retrieve the security prices from the MSN MoneyCentral web site.

Change a price. *If you enter an incorrect price, select the price from the Update Price dialog box's list box, and then click Delete.*

Manually Update the Prices in Your Portfolio

1 Display the Portfolio window.

2 Click Update Prices in the left pane.

3 Choose Update Price Manually from the menu.

4 Click the down arrow in the Investment field, and select the investment whose current market price you want to update.

5 Enter the current date.

6 Enter the current market price.

7 Click Update.

8 Repeat steps 4 through 7 for the other investments you're holding.

9 Click Close.

8

Recording Investment Purchases

After you've set up your investment accounts and described your current portfolio, you're ready to begin using Money for day-to-day record-keeping. Whenever you purchase more shares of a stock or mutual fund or additional bonds, you describe the purchase in the investment account's Account Register window.

TIP

Set up new investments. *If you haven't purchased the stock, bond, or mutual fund before, when you enter the name in the Investment field, Money displays the Create New Investment dialog box where you can set up the investment.*

Record a Purchase

1. Display the investment account register by clicking Investment Transactions in the left pane after opening the Account Summary.

2. Click New.

3. Enter the purchase date.

4. Enter a name for the investment, or select it from the list.

5. If this is the first time you've purchased this specific investment, Money displays two dialog boxes that you use to describe the investment in more detail.

6. Click the down arrow in the Activity field, and select Buy from the list.

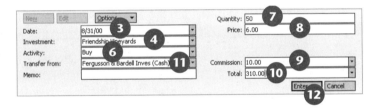

Describe a new purchase. *To describe a purchase or sale, you need to enter at least three of the following four inputs: Quantity, Price, Commission, and Total. If you leave one of these inputs blank, Money uses the other three inputs to calculate the fourth.*

7 Indicate the number of stock or mutual fund shares or the number of individual bonds you're purchasing.

8 Enter the dollar price per share or the price per bond.

9 Record any sales commission you paid.

10 Verify the contents of the Total field, and edit the value, if necessary, to correctly reflect the total purchase price.

11 Click the down arrow in the Transfer From field, and select the bank account or associated cash account you are using to pay for the purchase.

12 Click Enter.

Click an option button to identify the type of investment you're purchasing.

When you click Next, Money displays a second dialog box that asks you more detailed questions about the investment you're purchasing. The questions depend on the type of investment.

Recording Investment Sales

When you record the sale of an investment, you describe the transaction by following a series of steps similar to the steps you follow to purchase an investment.

TIP

Update annually. *For long-term investments such as retirement or college savings, wait until the end of the year to update your investment records. Then use the year-end statement to record a year's worth of distributions and reinvestment.*

Record a Sale

1. Display the investment account's register.

2. Click New.

3. Enter the sale date.

4. Click the down arrow in the Investment field, and select the name of the stock, bond, or mutual fund you're selling.

5. Click the down arrow in the Activity field, and select Sell from the list.

6. Enter the number of stock or mutual fund shares or the number of individual bonds you're selling.

7. Enter the price per share or price per bond you're receiving.

8. Record the commission you paid to sell the stock, bond, or mutual fund.

9. Verify the contents of the Total field, and edit the value if necessary, to reflect the total purchase amount.

10. Click the down arrow in the Transfer To field, and select the bank account or associated cash account in which you'll deposit the sale proceeds.

11. Click Enter.

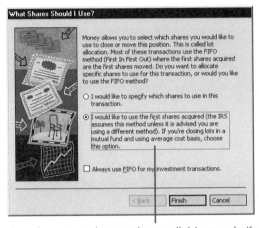

If you have more than one lot to sell, Money asks if you want to specify the lot. If you indicate that you do want to sell a lot other than the first one, click Next to specify the lot.

Recording Dividends and Distributions

Periodically, of course, you'll receive a mutual fund dividend distribution. Many stocks also pay dividends that you will have to record as well.

TIP

Distribution categories.
Select Interest from the Activity field for an interest distribution, Dividend for a dividend distribution, S-Term Cap Gains Dist for a short-term capital gains distribution, or L-Term Cap Gains for a long-term capital gains distribution.

TRY THIS

Generate a report.
Produce a Performance By Investment Account report or a Performance By Investment Type report to calculate the annual return you earn on investments. Click Investments in the left pane of the Report & Chart Gallery window, and then select the report you want to produce from the list.

Record Dividends

1. Display the investment account's register (Investment Transactions).

2. Click New.

3. Enter the dividend date.

4. Click the down arrow in the Investment field, and select the name of the stock or mutual fund that is distributing the dividend.

5. Click the down arrow in the Activity field, and select an entry from the list. For dividends from stocks, select Dividend.

6. Specify the amount of the dividend.

7. Click the down arrow in the Transfer To field, and select the bank account or associated cash account in which you'll deposit the dividend.

8. Click Enter.

Reinvesting Dividends and Distributions

With a mutual fund, you usually have the option of reinvesting the distributions you receive when the mutual fund returns a profit. By reinvesting, you continue to accumulate more shares. Typically, reinvested distributions aren't subject to the same sales commissions that regular purchases are. Some stock companies also offer shareholders the opportunity to buy more shares with their dividends. As with mutual funds, these dividend reinvestment programs, called DRIPs, let investors add to their holdings at a low cost because they typically don't require a brokerage commission.

TRY THIS

Calculate shares. *Fill out only the Price and Total fields, and Money calculates the quantity of shares.*

Reinvest Dividends or Distributions

1. Display the investment account register.

2. Click New.

3. Enter the reinvestment date.

4. Click the down arrow in the Investment field, and select the name of the investment.

5. Click the down arrow in the Activity field, and select an appropriate entry to describe the reinvestment. Select Reinvest Dividend for dividends from stocks.

6. Describe how many mutual fund shares you're purchasing by reinvesting the distribution.

7. Give the price per share you're paying for the new mutual fund shares.

8. Record any commission you paid to purchase the investment.

9. Verify the contents of the Total field, and edit the value, if necessary, so that it correctly reflects the total purchase amount.

10. Click Enter.

Select Reinvest Interest for a reinvested interest distribution, select Reinvest Dividend for a reinvested dividend distribution, select Reinvest S-Term CG Dist for a reinvested short-term capital gains distribution, or select Reinvest L-Term CG Dist for a reinvested long-term capital gains distribution.

Recording Other Income and Expenses

Money lets you record other income and expenses that don't fit into named categories. So if you have income that can't correctly be categorized as interest, dividends, or capital gains, you use the Other Income category. If you have an investment expense such as a brokerage account fee that you pay to maintain an account, use the Other Expense category.

TIP

When to leave Investment box empty. *If the income or expense amount is related only to the brokerage account in general, for example, and not to a specific investment, leave the Investment box empty.*

TIP

Record buys on margin. *If you buy stocks or bonds on margin, you record margin interest—the interest costs that your broker charges you on the borrowed money—as an Other Expense transaction.*

Record Other Income or Expenses

1 Display the investment account register.

2 Click New.

3 Enter the transaction date.

4 Click the down arrow in the Investment field, and select the name of the investment.

5 Click the down arrow in the Activity field, and select either Other Income or Other Expense.

6 Categorize the income or expense amount in the same way you would for a bank account transaction.

7 Enter the income or expense amount.

8 Click the down arrow in the Transfer From or Transfer To field, and select the account into which you'll deposit the income or from which you'll pay the expense.

9 Click Enter.

Recording Stock Splits

Companies whose share prices are growing quickly sometimes split shares of their stock to reduce the price per share, thereby making it easier for investors to buy even, one-hundred-share lots of the stock.

Record a Stock Split

1. Display the investment account register.

2. Click Manage Investments in the left pane.

3. Choose Record A Special Activity from the menu.

4. Choose Record A Split from the submenu.

5. Enter the stock split date.

6. Enter the number of new shares you're receiving.

7. Enter the number of old shares you had before the split.

8. Click OK.

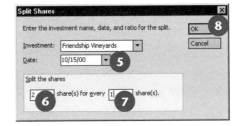

Recording Bond Interest

Bonds typically reward their holders by regularly paying interest. You record interest in the same way you record dividends and distributions for stocks and mutual funds.

TIP

Zero-coupon bonds. *Some bonds, such as zero-coupon bonds, don't pay interest over the course of their life. Instead, these bonds pay interest at the very end, when the bond is redeemed. See "Accrued Interest on Bonds" on page 132 for more information about how to treat zero-coupon bonds.*

TIP

Return of capital. *A return of capital is the return of a portion of the price you originally paid. To record a return of capital, or a liquidated dividend, select Return Of Capital from the Activity field. You know that a dividend is a return of capital because the statement you receive with the payment will identify it as such.*

Record Bond Interest

1. Display the investment account register.

2. Click New.

3. Enter the interest payment date.

4. Click the down arrow in the Investment field, and select the name of the bond paying the interest.

5. Click the down arrow in the Activity field, and select Interest.

6. Enter the amount of the interest payment.

7. Click the down arrow in the Transfer To field, and select the bank account or associated cash account in which you'll deposit the interest payment.

8. Click Enter.

Bond Premiums and Bond Discounts

If you pay more for a bond than the redemption price, the extra amount you pay is called a *premium*. You might ask, why would you and other investors pay more for a bond than the borrower will pay to redeem it? Because the borrower agrees to pay a higher rate of interest than the current rate. For example, imagine that a borrower issues $1,000 bonds that pay 6.6 percent interest, or $66. Subsequent to the issue of the bonds, investors like you decide that 6 percent is the going bond interest rate; a bond that pays $66 is therefore worth more than $1,000 because $66 is 6 percent of $1,100, not $1,000.

Bond premiums present an accounting problem. In effect, the $100 is an expense, or loss. Why? Although you might pay $1,100 for the bond described in the preceding paragraph, you only receive $1,000 when you redeem it.

For record-keeping purposes, you should spread the expense of the $100 bond premium over the years until the borrower redeems the bond. This is called amortization. To amortize the bond premium, multiply the effective interest rate the bond earns by its purchase price, and then subtract this amount from the actual interest the bond pays during the year. The difference is the bond premium expense that you will record the first year.

In the years that follow, you make only one minor modification in this bond-premium allocation formula. Instead of multiplying the effective interest rate the bond earns by the bond purchase price, you multiply the effective interest rate by the bond purchase price minus the bond premium amounts that you've already allocated.

Suppose, for example, that you purchase a $1,050 bond that pays an effective interest rate, or yield to maturity, of 6 percent. Further suppose that the bond pays $66 in interest annually. Given these facts, the bond premium charged as expense the first year would be calculated like this:

$$\$66 - (6\% \times \$1,050) = \$3$$

During the second year, the bond premium that is charged as an expense would be calculated as follows:

$$\$66 - [6\% \times (\$1,050 - \$3)] = \$3.18$$

During the third year, the bond premium charged as an expense would be calculated like so:

$$\$66 - [6\% \times (\$1,050 - \$3 - \$3.18)] = \$3.56$$

To record the allocations of bond premiums as expenses, you record two transactions. Record the bond premium allocation as an Other Expense for the bond, and specify the Transfer From account as the associated cash account. Record a return of capital transaction equal to the bond premium allocation, and specify the Transfer To account as the associated cash account.

Handling Bond Discounts

Bond discounts arise when buyers pay less for a bond than its redemption price. The difference between the purchase price and the redemption price is called the *discount*. A discount indicates that the borrower is paying less than the current rate.

Accounting for bond discounts works much like accounting for bond premiums. Suppose, for example, that a borrower issues a $1,000 bond that pays 6 percent interest, or $60, and that subsequent to the issue, investors decide that 6.66 percent should be the going rate. In this case, a bond that pays $60 is worth less than $1,000, because $60 is 6.66 percent of $900, not $1,000.

The $100 difference is income because, although you might pay $900 for the bond described in the preceding paragraph, you'll receive $1,000 when you redeem it. You should treat the $100 bond discount you receive as income and spread it over the years between the purchase and the redemption.

To make this discount allocation, you multiply the effective interest rate the bond earns by the bond purchase price and then subtract from this figure the actual interest the bond paid for the year. The difference is the bond discount income you record for the year. The effective interest rate is simply the yield to maturity—a figure you'll obtain when you purchase the bond.

In following years, you modify this bond-discount allocation formula by multiplying the effective interest rate by the bond purchase price plus the bond discount amounts already allocated.

Suppose that you purchase a $950 bond that pays an effective interest rate of 6.5 percent. This bond annually pays $60 in interest. Given these facts, the bond discount allocated as income the first year would be calculated like this:

$$(6.5\% \times \$950) - \$60 = \$1.75$$

During the second year, the bond discount allocated as income would be calculated as follows:

$$[6.5\% \times (\$950 + \$1.75)] - \$60 = \$1.86$$

During the third year, the bond discount allocated as income would be calculated like so:

$$[6.5\% \times (\$950 + \$1.75 + \$1.86)] - \$60 = \$1.98$$

To record the allocations of bond discounts as income, you treat the bond discount as accrued interest—which, in fact, is what it is. To do this, you first record the accrued bond interest (the bond discount allocation) as regular interest income. When you record this transaction, transfer the bond interest income to your associated cash account, even though there really won't be a deposit. (The interest will only accrue.) Then record a negative return of capital transaction equal to the accrued interest. When you record this second transaction, transfer the bond interest income out of your associated cash account. This way, Money records the interest income and adjusts the bond value for the accrued interest.

Accrued Interest on Bonds

Unless you buy or sell a bond on the interest payment day, some of what you pay when you buy the bond and some of what you receive when you sell it represents accrued interest. Accrued interest is simply the interest the bond has earned since the last interest payment date. Unfortunately, accrued interest increases both the work and the complexity of bond record-keeping.

Accrued Interest on Bonds You Purchase

To record the purchase of a bond with accrued interest, you record two transactions. For example, let's say you just purchased, for $1,020, a $1,000 bond with $20 of accrued interest. First, record the purchase of the actual bond without the accrued interest: $1,000. Then record a return of capital transaction with a negative return of capital amount equal to the accrued interest (in this case, $20). At this point, Money shows your bond's value as equal to $1,020.

When you get your next interest payment—let's say it's $60—you record two transactions: a return of capital transaction equal to $20 and an interest income transaction equal to $40. In this way, you don't count as income the $20 of accrued interest you actually paid when you purchased the bond. And you record as interest income only the $40 you actually earned.

Accrued Interest on Bonds You Own

Some bonds accrue interest but don't pay the interest. (The bond issuer typically reports this accrued but unpaid interest on form 1099-OID at the end of the year.) To keep a good record of these bonds, you need to record the accrued interest annually because the interest income is taxable. To do this, you record two transactions. First, you record the accrued bond interest as regular interest income. When you record this transaction, transfer the bond interest income to your associated cash account—even though there really won't be a deposit because the interest will only accrue. Then record a negative return of capital transaction equal to the accrued interest. When you record this second transaction, transfer the bond interest income from your associated cash account. In this way, Money records the interest income and adjusts the bond value for the accrued interest.

Real Estate Investing

9

Many investors prize real estate because it is a hedge against inflation and because many types of real estate investments deliver solid cash returns. Real estate investments present unusual record-keeping challenges, however, both for passive real estate investors and for active real estate investors.

Passive real estate investors put their money into real estate investments they don't actively manage, such as limited partnership units or shares and real estate investment trusts (REITs). While that sounds straightforward, recording the income and expenses of passive real estate investments is unfortunately more complicated than, say, recording the income and expenses that pertain to stocks or bonds. (Don't worry if you don't understand this lingo yet—I'll go into more detail in a minute.)

Active real estate investors actually buy, sell, and manage their real estate investments, treating their investments as, essentially, a business. Not surprisingly, then, active real estate investments require you to set up business bookkeeping systems. Despite these challenges, Microsoft Money 2000 provides real estate investors with a wonderful set of tools and possibilities.

Creating Passive Real Estate Investment Accounts

Passive real estate investments include limited partnership units and shares in real estate investment trusts. At first glance, these investments resemble stocks, but they actually work quite differently because not all the cash you receive comes in the form of interest or dividends. Typically, a substantial portion of the distributions from a passive real estate investment represents a return of capital.

Despite their complexity, however, you can use Money to keep accurate financial records of passive real estate investments.

What do you want to do?

Add a new account
Track activity for a new bank account, credit card, loan, investment, or asset.

Set Up a Passive Real Estate Investment Account

1. Click Accounts on the navigation bar to display the Account Manager window.

2. Click Set Up Accounts in the left pane.

3. Click Add A New Account. Money starts the New Account Wizard.

4. Optionally, enter the name of the financial institution associated with the account, and click Next.

5. Select the appropriate institution name from the list of names Money found that matched the institution you entered, or click Next to use the name exactly how you entered it.

6. Select Investment from the list of accounts, and click Next.

7. Enter a name for the investment account, and select the currency the account uses.

8. Specify whether the account is tax deferred by selecting the appropriate option, and click Next.

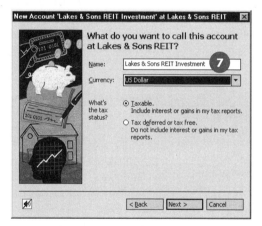

The best way to start investing in real estate.

Invest in your own home. On average, home ownership investment has delivered returns roughly equal to those of the stock market. Note, however, that it's difficult to make money on any real estate investment—including the purchase of a home—unless you hold the investment for a lengthy period of time. Typically, you need several years of appreciation just to pay for the selling costs.

9 Click the No I'll Do This Later option button to answer the question about whether you want to describe each of the investments in your account. Then click Next.

10 Enter the estimated value of the investments in the account. Or, optionally, just leave this blank if you don't know or aren't sure.

11 If the investment has an associated cash account, enter the cash account's ending balance from your last monthly statement and click Next.

12 If a financial institution is associated with the account, Money asks whether you have any other accounts to set up. Click the I Have No Other Accounts At This Institution option button, and click Next.

13 Click Finish.

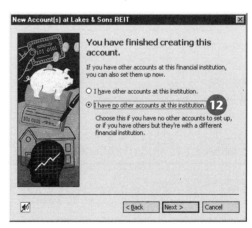

Recording Real Estate Investment Purchases

Whenever you purchase partnership units or shares in a real estate investment trust, you need to describe the purchase in the investment account's Account Register window. The process of recording a passive real estate investment purchase is the same as the process for recording a stock, bond, or mutual fund purchase.

Investment Transactions

TIP

Choose an investment type. *Not all types of transactions are available for all investment types. If you need to collect interest as well as dividends, for example, you may want to choose the Mutual Fund investment type instead of the Stock investment type for the most flexibility.*

Record a Passive Real Estate Investment Purchase

1. Display the investment account register.

2. Click New.

3. Enter the purchase date.

4. Enter a name for the investment. If you haven't purchased units or shares of the real estate partnership or investment trust before, Money displays the Create New Investment dialog box.

5. Select the stock or investment type option that most closely matches your investment, click Next, and then click Finish.

6. Click the down arrow in the Activity field, and select Buy from the list.

7. Enter the number of partnership units or trust shares you're purchasing.

8. Enter the price per unit or share you're paying.

Passive real estate investments. *In a passive real estate investment, you don't actively manage the investment. For example, you don't pick a property manager, collect rent, or arrange financing. If you purchased shares of a real estate investment trust (REIT) or invested in a real estate project as a limited partner, your investment is probably passive.*

Publicly traded investments. *If you're describing a publicly traded real estate investment and you intend to use Money's Online Quotes feature, you need to enter the security symbol in the Create New Investment dialog box. See "Using Online Quotes" on page 119 for more information.*

⑨ Record any sales commission you paid.

⑩ Verify the contents of the Total field, and edit the value, if necessary, so that it correctly reflects the total purchase amount.

⑪ Click the down arrow in the Transfer From field, and select the bank account or associated cash account you're using to purchase the investment. Keep this box blank if you're recording a past purchase.

⑫ Click Enter.

Create New Investment: Mbone

What type of investment is it?

○ Mutual Fund (including those that invest in stocks, bonds and/or index fund)

⊙ Stock (common, preferred, and options) ⑤

○ Certificates of Deposit/US Savings Bond (including series EE and HH)

○ Money Market

○ Bond (including treasuries, corporate bonds, municipal bonds and zero-coupon bonds)

○ Employee Stock Option Grant

Next >   Cancel

9

Recording Real Estate Investment Sales

When you sell units or shares of a real estate investment, of course, you describe that transaction too. You record the sale of a real estate investment in the same way that you record the sale of a stock or mutual fund shares or individual bonds.

Record a Real Estate Investment Sale

1. Display the investment account register, and click New.

2. Enter the sale date.

3. Identify the name of the real estate investment you're selling.

4. Click the down arrow in the Activity field, and select Sell from the list.

5. Describe how many partnership units or trust shares you're selling.

6. Enter the price per share or per unit you're receiving.

7. Record any sales commission you paid to sell the units or shares.

8. Verify the contents of the Total field, and edit the value, if necessary, to correctly reflect the total purchase amount.

9. Click the down arrow in the Transfer To field, and select the bank account or associated cash account in which you'll deposit the sale proceeds.

10. Click Enter.

Recording Real Estate Investment Distributions

At the end of the quarter or the end of the year, you usually receive a real estate investment fund dividend distribution, which you then need to record.

TIP

Other transactions.
Select Interest for an interest distribution, Dividend for a dividend distribution, S-Term Cap Gains Dist for a short-term capital gains distribution, L-Term Cap Gains for a long-term capital gains distribution, or Other Income, depending on what investment type you chose.

TIP

Distribution types.
The quarterly or year-end distribution statement you receive identifies the type of distribution. You don't have to worry about making this determination.

Record a Real Estate Investment Distribution

1. Display the investment account register, and click New.

2. Enter the distribution date.

3. Click the down arrow in the Investment field, and select the investment fund making the distribution.

4. Click the down arrow in the Activity field, and select an entry from the list.

5. Specify the amount of the distribution.

6. Click the down arrow in the Transfer To field, and select the bank account or associated cash account in which you'll deposit the distribution.

7. Click Enter to record the distribution.

9

Recording Return of Capital Transactions

Sometimes a distribution isn't a share of the real estate profits but a return of capital—a return of a portion of the price you originally paid. Recording a return of capital for real estate investments works the same way as it does for stocks and bonds.

Record a Return of Capital Transaction

1. Display the investment account register.

2. Click New.

3. Enter the return of capital date.

4. Click the down arrow in the Investment field, and select the investment.

5. Click the down arrow in the Activity field, and select Return Of Capital from the list.

6. Enter the amount of the capital return.

7. Click the down arrow in the Transfer To field, and select the bank account or associated cash account in which you'll deposit the return of capital.

8. Click Enter.

Setting Up Real Estate Property Accounts

If you're an active real estate investor, you can also use Money to simplify and expedite your record-keeping. In essence, you'll use Money to track three things: the adjusted cost basis of your properties, the mortgages associated with any of your properties, and the income and expenses that individual properties produce. To track the adjusted cost basis of your investments, first set up asset accounts for each individual property you own.

SEE ALSO

See "When to Repay and Refinance Mortgages" on pages 110–111 for information about making mortgage-refinancing decisions.

Set Up an Active Real Estate Investment Account

1. Click Accounts on the navigation bar to display the Account Manager window.

2. Click Set Up Accounts in the left pane.

3. Click the Add A New Account hyperlink.

4. Leave the Bank or Financial Institution field empty, and click Next.

5. Select Asset from the list of accounts, and click Next.

6. Enter a name for the asset account, enter the date you set up the account, and click Next.

7. Enter the original purchase price of the property.

8. Money asks whether a loan is associated with the investment. Select the appropriate option, and click Next.

9. If a loan is associated with the investment, enter the name of the loan account.

10. Click Finish.

9

Building a Real Estate Investment Category List

To keep records of an individual property's income and expenses, you do two very simple things. First, you create a list of categories specifically for tracking your real estate investments. Second, you use these real estate income and expense categories to record transactions related to your real estate investments.

TIP

Use Schedule E. *Although you can use any list of income or expense categories you want, you should base your categories on Schedule E of the federal income tax form, which you use to report your real estate profits or losses to the federal government.*

Add a Real Estate Income or Expense Category

1. Click More on the navigation bar, and then choose Categories & Payees from the menu.

2. Click New.

3. Click the Create A New Category option button, and click Next.

4. Enter a name for the new real estate category.

5. Specify whether the new category is an income or expense category by selecting the appropriate option, and then click Next.

6. Select a general group to describe the new category from the list, and click Finish.

7. Repeat steps 2 through 6 to add each of the income and expense categories you need.

Setting Up Property Classifications

If you own more than one piece of property, you'll also want to create classifications to track each property's income and expenses. To create property classifications, first turn on the classification feature, and then create a classification for each property you own.

TIP

Properties field. *Once you create a Properties classification, the Properties field shows up in the transaction forms for all your asset, bank, and cash accounts.*

TRY THIS

Use the street address. *You may want to use a property's street address as its classification name.*

Turn on the Classification Feature

1. Click More on the navigation bar, and then choose Categories & Payees from the menu.

2. Click Classification 1 in the left pane.

3. Click the Properties option button.

4. Click OK.

Create Property Classifications

1. Click More on the navigation bar, and then choose Categories & Payees from the menu.

2. Click Properties in the left pane.

3. Click New.

4. Enter the name of the real estate investment.

5. Click OK.

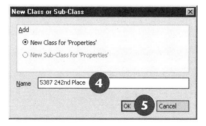

9

Tracking the Adjusted Cost of Property

Once you set up an asset account, you can use it to track improvements you make to the property (because improvements increase the property's adjusted cost) and your annual depreciation (because depreciation decreases the property's adjusted cost). The adjusted cost basis of a property is important. When you some day sell the property, you calculate the capital gain or loss by subtracting the adjusted cost from the net sales price.

Record Depreciation

1. Display the real estate property's asset account register.

2. Click the Decrease tab, and if necessary, click New.

3. Enter the date for the asset depreciation transaction.

4. Optionally, enter a description of the asset depreciation in the Pay To field.

5. Enter the amount of the annual depreciation charge.

6. Type *Depreciation* in the Category field. If you have not recorded depreciation before, Money displays the New Category dialog box. Click Next, optionally select a category to place it under, and then click Finish.

7. Classify the real estate investment in the Properties field.

8. Click Enter.

Depreciate per year. *If you're entering a series of annual depreciation transactions, use a different year in the Date field for each transaction so that they get counted in a different year's profit or loss calculation.*

Capital improvement vs. repairs and maintenance. *When you spend money fixing up a real estate property, you need to determine whether the expenditure is a capital improvement or a repairs and maintenance expense. You add capital improvement expenditures to the property's asset account, thereby increasing the adjusted cost. You use repairs and maintenance expenditures only to calculate the current year's profit or loss. It typically makes more sense to call an expenditure a repairs and maintenance expense than it does to call it a capital improvement. You can't make this decision yourself, however. The IRS has specific guidelines about what does and doesn't constitute a capital improvement. The general rule, however, is that if an expenditure adds to a property's useful life or its functionality, it's a capital improvement.*

Record a Capital Improvement

1. Display the register for the bank account or associated cash account you'll use to pay for the capital improvements.

2. Click the Withdrawal tab, and if necessary, click New.

3. Enter the check number.

4. Enter the check date.

5. Enter the name of the person or business you're paying.

6. Enter the check amount.

7. Click the down arrow in the Category field, and select Transfer from the list.

8. Click the down arrow in the Subcategory field, and select the name of the property account.

9. Classify the real estate investment in the Properties field.

10. Enter a memo describing the improvement in detail.

11. Click Enter.

Recording Real Estate Income and Expense Transactions

After you've created a list of income and expense categories, keep your checkbook as usual—except when you record an income or expense related to a real estate property. Then you use the appropriate real estate income or expense category and describe the real estate investment using the Properties fields.

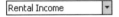

Record Real Estate Income

① Display the register for the bank account or associated cash account in which you want to deposit the real estate income.

② Click the Deposit tab, and if necessary, click New.

③ Enter the check number.

④ Enter the deposit date.

⑤ Enter the name of the person or business that paid you.

⑥ Enter the amount of the check.

⑦ Click the down arrow in the Category field, and select a real estate income category that describes the deposit.

⑧ Click the down arrow in the Properties field, and select the real estate property's classification.

⑨ Click Enter.

SEE ALSO

See Section 3, "Keeping Your Checkbook," for more information on using bank accounts.

Record Real Estate Expense

1. Display the register for the bank account or associated cash account from which you want to pay for the real estate expense.

2. Click the Withdrawal tab, and if necessary, click New.

3. Enter the check number.

4. Enter the date.

5. Enter the name of the person or business you're paying.

6. Enter the amount of the check.

7. Click the down arrow in the Category field, and select a real estate expense category that describes the expenditure.

8. Click the down arrow in the Properties field, and select the real estate property's classification.

9. Click Enter.

Reporting on Active Real Estate Investments

Once you collect income and expense data for active real estate investments, it's easy to create a report that summarizes income and expense data by property.

TRY THIS

Use for Schedule E. *Use this Income vs. Spending report to get most of the data you need to complete the Schedule E form.*

Produce a Real Estate Investment Report

1. Click Reports on the navigation bar.

2. Click Spending Habits in the left pane.

3. Select Income vs. Spending from the list.

4. Click Go To Report/Chart.

5. Click Customize to display the Customize Report dialog box.

6. Click the Rows & Columns tab, click the down arrow in the Columns field, and select Properties from the list.

7. Click OK to update the Income vs. Spending report using different columns to show income and spending by real estate investment.

Choosing Appropriate Real Estate Investment Categories

The following figure shows the standard income and expense categories from the 1998 Schedule E form used to report supplemental income from rental real estate. These categories can change from year to year. If you can't get a newer form, however, this outdated form is a good one to base your categories in Money on because you need to begin tracking income and expenses at the start of the year, before the new Schedule E form for the current year comes out. Although you can't be certain that the categories you use in Money will match the form you'll have to use, you'll probably not be far off.

Income:		Properties				Totals (Add columns A, B, and C.)	
		A	B	C			
3 Rents received	3					3	
4 Royalties received	4					4	
Expenses:							
5 Advertising	5						
6 Auto and travel (see page E-2) .	6						
7 Cleaning and maintenance . . .	7						
8 Commissions	8						
9 Insurance	9						
10 Legal and other professional fees	10						
11 Management fees	11						
12 Mortgage interest paid to banks, etc. (see page E-2)	12					12	
13 Other interest	13						
14 Repairs	14						
15 Supplies	15						
16 Taxes	16						
17 Utilities	17						
18 Other (list) ▶...................							
....							
....	18						
....							

10

Online Banking, Bill Payment, and Web Browsing

One way to take advantage of the power of emerging online technologies is by using one or both of Microsoft Money 2000's online service features:

◆ Online Bill Payment

◆ Online Statements

You might have read an article or two about home banking and how it will revolutionize the way people interact with their banks. More and more banks now offer some sort of online services. Users of version 3 of Microsoft Money had only three banks in the entire country to choose from if they wanted to bank online. Now hundreds of banks participate, including many of the largest in the country.

You can use one or both of Money's online services. The services are tightly integrated into the program and require no additional software. To use either of the services, however, you do need an Internet connection. And to use online statements, you need to hold an account at a participating bank.

Setting Up New Internet Connections

The integration of Internet Explorer and Money allows you to complete a wide array of online tasks directly from the Money program window. If you've never used Internet Explorer 5 before, you need to first set up the program to work with your modem and Internet service provider connection. You need to do this if you want to take advantage of any of Money's online features, even if you're not planning to download statements or pay bills online.

> **TIP**
>
> **Set up an existing connection.** *To customize your connection settings in Money, choose Connection Settings from the Tools menu and use the boxes and buttons on the Connections tab to specify an existing Internet connection to use and when you want to connect.*

Find an Internet Service Provider

1. Make sure your modem is plugged in, turned on, and connected to your phone line.

2. Choose Connection Settings from the Tools menu.

3. Click Setup to start the Internet Connection Wizard.

4. Click the first option button, and click Next. The Internet Connection Wizard dials a toll-free number and then displays a list of Internet service providers in your area.

5. Select a service, and click Next to sign up for an account. Fill out the personal information the wizard requests, and click Next to display a web page run by the Internet service provider.

6. Follow the Internet service provider's instructions to continue applying for an account.

Update Internet information. *To update the headlines and information on your Money Home Page and to update stock prices all at once, choose Update Internet Information from the Tools menu.*

Set Up a New Internet Connection Manually

1 Choose Connection Settings from the Tools menu.

2 Click Setup to start the Internet Connection Wizard.

3 Click the third option button, and click Next.

4 Tell Money whether you connect to the Internet over a local area network or by using a dial-up connection.

5 If you're setting up a dial-up connection, select the modem you want to use for the connection, enter the phone number, enter your user name and password, and enter a name for the connection in the wizard's dialog boxes.

6 Proceed through the wizard to set up new Internet mail, news, and directory service accounts if necessary.

7 Click Finish.

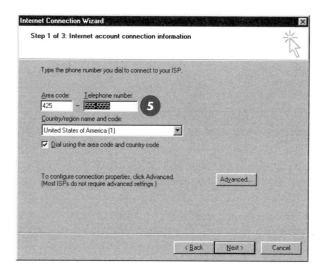

Setting Up Online Services

Once you have an Internet connection set up, you can set up online services in Money. With Online Statements, you can download your bank statements and transactions and transfer money between online accounts. With Online Bill Payment, you can send checks electronically.

TIP

Create an online account.
If you haven't yet created the account for which you want to use Money's online services, click Set Up Accounts in the left pane of the Accounts Place and click the Add A New Account hyperlink. See "Setting Up Bank Accounts" on page 16 for more information about creating bank accounts.

Set Up Online Statements and Bill Payment

1. Click Accounts on the navigation bar, and click Set Up Accounts in the left pane.

2. Click the Set Up Online Services hyperlink.

3. Select the account for which you want to set up online services.

4. Click Set Up.

5. Select your bank from the drop-down list box, and click Next.

6. Verify the name of the bank, and click Next.

7. If you have your sign-up information from your bank, click the first option button and click Next twice. If you do not, click the second option button and click Next twice to investigate the online offerings at your bank. Before you can set up an account for online services in Money, you must apply for the services with your bank and receive the setup instructions from them.

8. Enter your name, address, phone number, and Social Security number in the boxes provided.

9. If you have more than one account at the bank, select the account you want to set up and click Next.

10. Select the online services you want to set up, and click Next.

11. Enter the account number, account type, and the routing number, and click Next.

12. Specify whether you want to set up another account, and click Next.

13. Click Finish when you've completed setting up your accounts for online services.

10

Downloading Bank Account Records

Before you can use online banking services, you must have an account set up at a participating bank. Then once you're set up, you can easily download statements from your bank, transfer money between accounts, and even order new checks. Downloading your statements is a cinch. It involves two steps: downloading the records and adding the downloaded transactions to your account register.

Download Bank Account Records

1 Click Accounts on the navigation bar, and click Get Online Statements in the left pane.

2 Click Connect To All.

3 Enter your password in the Password box.

4 By default, Money attempts to download statements for all online accounts. If you don't want to download a statement, click it and click the Don't Send On Next Call option button.

5 Click Connect. You'll see a series of messages as your computer sends and receives information.

6 Confirm that the call was completed successfully, and click Close.

Account balances don't match. *Don't worry if the downloaded account balance you see on the screen differs from the balance you see in the account register. The amounts will probably differ because the balance in your account register reflects all transactions, including those that have not cleared the bank (even those scheduled to take place in the future), whereas the balance from your bank does not.*

View Bank Account Records

1 Click Accounts on the navigation bar, and click Get Online Statements in the left pane.

2 Click View Downloaded Balances in the left pane.

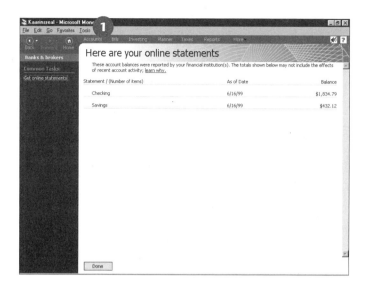

Making Electronic Payments

With Money's Online Bill Payment service, you can pay any business or individual in the United States right from your computer. The service works with any checking account in the United States, and the suggested retail price is $4.95 per month for 20 payments. Additional payments are usually about $.50 each.

Enter an Electronic Payment

1 Display the register for the account you've set up for online services.

2 Click the Withdrawal tab, or if the Withdrawal tab is currently displayed, click New.

3 Click the down arrow in the Number field, and select Epay from the list.

4 Enter the date you want the payment delivered (or the payment's due date).

5 Enter the name of the payee. This name will appear on the envelope and the Pay To line of the check. If you've never made out a check to this payee, Money will display the Online Payee Details dialog box, asking for the payee's contact information.

6 Make sure this is the way you want the payee's name to appear on the check and the envelope.

7 Enter the address, including the five- or nine-digit zip code of the payee. Use the second line of the street address field, if necessary.

Enter once. *You only have to enter information once for each payee.*

Send payment reminders. *If you have created an electronic payment but have not yet sent it to the Online Bill Payment service, Money displays a reminder on the Money Home Page and in the account register.*

Spot an electronic payment. *Once you enter a transaction, an open envelope icon and a lighting bolt icon appear in the Number field of the account register. The lightning bolt means that it's an electronic payment. The open envelope means that you haven't sent the payment yet.*

8. Optionally, enter the phone number of the payee. Although this is not required, it's a good idea in case there is a problem with the payment.

9. If the payment is going to a business with which you have an account, such as the phone company, enter your account number.

10. Click OK to return to the register.

11. Enter the amount of the payment.

12. Categorize the payment.

13. Enter a memo.

14. Click Enter.

10

Sending Electronic Payments

Once you enter all your electronic payments, the next step is to send them to the online services. Then the check is cut so that it can be sent through the mail to the payee.

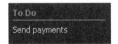

To Do

Send payments

TRY THIS

Send a payment from the register. *If you have an electronic payment entered but not yet sent and you're in the account register, you can click Send Payments in the left pane and send the payment.*

Send an Electronic Payment

1. Click Accounts on the navigation bar.

2. Click Send Payments in the left pane.

3. Review the payment information you entered. If you subscribe to the Online Statements service, you'll also see instructions for updating the statement and balance of your Online Statements accounts.

4. Enter your password.

5. Click Connect. You'll see a progression of messages as your payment is sent and received.

6. Confirm that the transaction was completed successfully, and click Close.

Cancel an unsent payment.
*If you haven't yet sent the
electronic payment (if it still
says "Epay" next to the open
envelope icon in the Number
field of the account register),
you can cancel it by selecting it
and pressing the Delete key.*

TIP

**Check the status of an
electronic payment.** *To see
the status of an electronic
payment you've made in the
last 60 days, click Accounts on
the navigation bar and click
the hyperlink for the bank to
which you sent the instructions
at the bottom of the Accounts
Place. Then click the Status Of
Electronic Payments hyperlink.*

Cancel an Electronic Payment

1. Display the account register with the electronic payment you want to cancel.

2. Right-click the transaction you want to cancel, and choose Mark As from the shortcut menu and Void from the submenu.

3. Click the Yes option button when Money asks whether you want to create an instruction to cancel the payment.

4. Click Connect To Bank in the left pane.

5. Choose Connect To Online Services from the menu.

6. Make sure the cancel payment instruction is there, and enter your password if necessary.

7. Click Connect to send the cancellation instruction to the bank.

10

Making Automatic Payments

If you want to take the convenience of online bill payment one step further, you can also tell the Online Bill Payment service to make payments for you automatically so you don't have to remember to connect to your bank to send the payment instruction. This works only for recurring payments of a fixed amount, such as rent, car, and mortgage payments. When you authorize an automatic payment, the checks are sent weekly, monthly, bimonthly, or at whatever frequency you specify.

Create an Automatic Payment

1 Click Bills on the navigation bar, and click New.

2 Click the Bill option button, and click Next.

3 Select the online account from which you pay the bill.

4 Enter the date for the first payment.

5 Enter the name of the person or business you are paying.

6 Enter the amount of the payment.

7 Categorize the payment, and click Next.

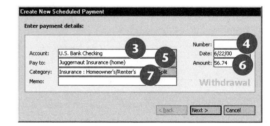

Set up automatic payments carefully. *Once you set up automatic payments, the payments are made whether or not you connect to the online services.*

Monthly automatic payments. *If you are creating a monthly automatic payment, the payment will be delivered on the same day of each month.*

Automatic payment reminders. *One month before an automatic payment is due, it will be downloaded to your account register as a reminder that it's coming up. Once it has been downloaded, you can make any changes you want (including canceling the payment).*

8 Click the More Than Once option button, select how often the bill comes due from the Frequency field, and then click Next.

9 Select Electronic Payment (Epay) from the Payment Method drop-down list box, and click Next.

10 Specify whether the payment is a constant amount or whether it varies, and click Next.

11 Specify whether or not you want Money to record the first payment, and click Finish.

10

Canceling Automatic Payments

You have two options for canceling an automatic payment. You can cancel an individual occurrence of the payment but keep the automatic payment in your payment calendar for the future, or you can delete all occurrences of the payment.

TIP

Delete an individual automatic payment. *You can also delete an individual automatic payment from within the Bills area by right-clicking the automatic payment and choosing Skip Transaction from the shortcut menu. Then connect to your bank to send the cancellation instruction.*

Cancel an Individual Automatic Payment

1. In the online account's register, right-click the transaction you want to cancel.

2. Choose Mark As from the shortcut menu, and then choose Void from the submenu.

3. Click Connect To Bank in the left pane.

4. Choose Connect To Online Services from the menu.

5. Make sure the cancel payment instruction is there, and enter your password if necessary.

6. Click Connect to send the cancellation instruction to the bank.

Permanently Cancel an Automatic Payment

1 Click Bills on the navigation bar.

2 Click Setup Bills & Deposits in the left pane.

3 Select the automatic payment you want to cancel, and click Delete.

4 Click Yes to confirm the delete.

5 Click Accounts on the navigation bar.

6 Click the bank's hyperlink in the list of Financial Institutions at the bottom of the page.

7 Click the Connect To Online Services hyperlink, and review the instructions to cancel the automatic payment.

8 Click Connect.

10

Transferring Money Online

As long as you have two accounts at the same bank and both are registered for the Online Statements service, you can electronically transfer money between them.

TIP

Use today's date. *For electronic transfers, you must use today's date. The transfer takes place at the end of the day. If you request an electronic transfer after the cut-off time, it is processed at the end of the following business day. Transfers to and from credit card accounts have an additional one-day delay.*

TRY THIS

Confirm transfers. *Check your statement on the day following the transfer to make sure the money was transferred.*

Transfer Money Between Accounts

1. Display the register for the online account from which you want to transfer money.

2. Click the Transfer tab.

3. Click Common Transfers, and choose Electronic Transfer (Xfer) from the menu.

4. Click the down arrow in the From field, and select the name of the account from which you're transferring the money.

5. Enter the transfer date.

6. Click the down arrow in the To field, and select the name of the account to which you're transferring money.

7. Enter the amount you want transferred between the accounts.

8. Click Enter.

9. Connect to your bank to send the transfer instruction.

Sending E-Mail to Your Bank

You can send electronic mail, or e-mail, to your bank to inquire about a payment, request a copy of a check, order new paper checks, or send a general-purpose letter.

Write Letter...

TRY THIS

See your bank's contact information. *Click your bank's hyperlink at the bottom of the Accounts Place, and click the hyperlink under View Contact Information.*

TIP

Delete a letter. *To delete a letter you have written, click the letter's hyperlink in the Connect dialog box and click the Never Send This Transaction option button.*

Send an E-Mail Message to Your Bank

1. Click Accounts on the navigation bar.

2. Click the hyperlink for the bank to which you want to send a message from the bottom of the Accounts Place.

3. Click the Create Instructions For hyperlink for the bank.

4. Click Write Letter.

5. Select the option that corresponds to the type of letter you want to send, and click Continue.

6. Write the letter.

7. Click OK.

8. Click Connect to send the letter.

10

Researching Personal Finance Topics on the Internet

The Internet is the richest source of all types of personal financial information. Unfortunately, it's also the most disorganized. There isn't a single place to go to get all the information you want. You can get personal finance information from newsgroups, from mailing list messages, and on World Wide Web sites.

I'm not going to describe how to use all these features here because the procedure differs depending on your Internet service provider, on the web browser you use, and on your e-mail client software. For purposes of this discussion, therefore, I assume you already have access to the Internet. So in this section, I'll tell you specifically where to locate personal finance information.

Newsgroups

An Internet *newsgroup* is really just an electronic bulletin board. Some people post messages on the bulletin board, and other people read them. A handful of newsgroups post messages on personal financial topics. As long as you have a newsgroup reader (such as Microsoft Outlook Express, which comes as a part of Internet Explorer on the Money 2000 CD-ROM) and access to the Internet or to an online service that hosts newsgroups, you can read the posted messages and even post your own.

At the time I am writing this, the following public newsgroups are available and active.

NEWSGROUP NAME	WHAT IT COVERS
aus.invest	Investments in Australia or of special interest to Australians
microsoft.public.investor	All types of investment discussion
microsoft.public.money	Tips and troubleshooting advice by Microsoft Money users
misc.invest	All types of investment discussion
misc.invest.canada	Investments in Canada or of special interest to Canadians
misc.invest.funds	Mutual fund investing
misc.invest.real-estate	Real estate investing
misc.invest.stocks	Common stock investments
misc.invest.stocks.penny	Penny stocks
misc.invest.technical	Technical analysis (charting) of securities
soc.college.financial-aid	Help finding and applying for financial aid
uk.finance	General finance information especially targeted for residents of the United Kingdom

Mailing Lists

Internet *mailing lists* are simply lists of electronic mail addresses. When someone mails a message to the mailing list, everyone whose name is on the list gets the message. This might seem like much ado about nothing, but because mailing lists cater to the interests of their members, mailing lists are powerful communication tools. Several Internet mailing lists provide useful personal information.

You can get a list of mailing lists organized by subject by visiting the web site at *www.liszt.com*. This web site also lists the instructions for subscribing to each of the mailing lists.

World Wide Web Sites

The Internet provides hundreds of popular World Wide Web sites related to personal finance, including the online versions of several popular financial newspapers and magazines. Some sites are free; others require you to subscribe. One site you might be interested in is that of the *Wall Street Journal* at *www.wsj.com*.

Another way to find web sites related to the personal finance topic you're interested in is by using a search service such as Yahoo! at *www.yahoo.com*. You can use the search service of your choice to enter a personal finance word or phrase and build a list of web sites falling under that category or including the text you entered.

Your Online Service Provider

In a general sense, online services such as America Online, CompuServe, Prodigy, and The Microsoft Network work the same way. Each provides up-to-the-minute news and delayed stock prices, special online columns and newsletters that cover personal financial topics, and personal financial chat rooms and bulletin boards where you can ask questions about investing. Most of the services also let you connect to online brokerage services.

Compared with haphazardly searching the web, these online services provide a unique advantage. Usually, you can simply click a button, and the service displays a list of the personal financial or investing features it provides. The service often also lets you designate or customize your start page to list your investments.

10

Using Money Web Express

Money 2000 allows you to make transactions and access your financial information from any personal computer with Internet access. With Roaming Register, you can make online bill payments from a different location. With Roaming Portfolio, you can record investment purchases. You can also get financial news and view your budget. Money Web Express works by allowing you to store Money data on the Internet and then access it using a password. To set up Money Web Express, click Investing on the navigation bar, click the Access My Money Data On The Web hyperlink and then click Set Up Roaming.

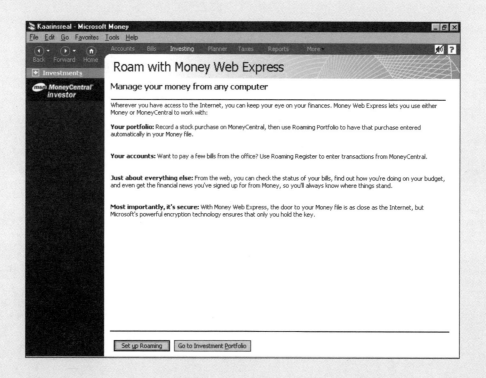

The Money Web Page

The Money web page is a great way to quickly access technical support with Money and get the latest product information and tips for Money users. From this page, you can also link to a wealth of personal financial resources and even send Microsoft Corporation any comments or suggestions you have for improving the program.

> **TIP**
>
> **Access the Money web page without opening Money.** *You can also access the Money web page just as you would open any other web page in your web browser. Simply enter the address* www.microsoft.com/Money/.

> **TIP**
>
> **The Money web page changes.** *Your screen will look a little different from the figure on this page because Microsoft constantly updates the web page for Money.*

Access the Money Web Page

1. Choose Microsoft On The Web from the Help menu, and choose Microsoft Money Home Page from the submenu.

2. Click a hyperlink to access the information you need.

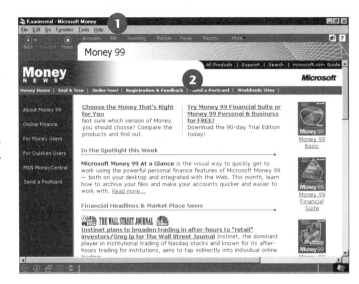

11

Managing a Small Business with Money

Although Microsoft Money 2000 is chiefly a personal finance program, it is also perfectly suited for keeping financial records for many small businesses. Before you start using Money for small business accounting, however, you need to think about whether Money will work for you. Here's a breakdown of what Money can and cannot do. Use this list to determine whether Money will meet your needs or if you should instead upgrade to a complete small business accounting program.

Tasks you can generally complete with any version of Money:

- ◆ Print checks for a business

- ◆ Track business bank accounts and business investments

- ◆ Prepare payroll for salaried employees

Tasks generally beyond the scope of Money:

- ◆ Print business forms such as invoices (except if you have the Business & Personal version of Money)

- ◆ Track inventory, accounts payable accounts, and loans payable accounts

- ◆ Calculate payroll expenses, depreciation, and bid amounts

- ◆ Track owner's equity

Adding Business Income and Expense Categories

Before you can start keeping your books with Money, you need to set up the bank account in which you'll make business transactions. Then you need to create categories to track your business income and expenses. Although you can create your own categories, you'll want to use the categories that are on the Schedule C business tax return.

TIP

Distinquish business from personal. *If you're using the same category list to track business and personal expenses, you may want to start each category name with the word Business or the abbreviation Bus to identify it as a business category.*

Add an Income or Expense Category

1. Click More on the navigation bar, and then choose Categories & Payees from the menu.

2. Click the Categories hyperlink in the left pane.

3. Click New.

4. Click the Create A New Category option button, and click Next.

5. Enter a name for the business income or expense category.

6. Specify whether the new category is an income or an expense category by selecting the appropriate option, and then click Next.

7. Indicate that an income category falls into the Other Income group, or indicate that an expense category falls into the Other Expense group.

8. Click Finish.

9. Repeat steps 2 through 8 to add all the business income and business expense categories you need.

Identifying the Tax Treatment of a Category

After you add an income or expense category, you need to describe how Money should treat the category for income tax purposes. Specifically, you need to identify where the category is reported for income tax purposes.

TIP

Which tax form? *If you don't know which form you'll use at the end of the year—Schedule C or Schedule C-EZ—specify the Schedule C-EZ form.*

TIP

Separate business categories. *If you'll use Money to keep track of more than one business's books, each business needs to use its own set of categories.*

Describe the Tax Treatment of a Category

1. Click More on the navigation bar, and then choose Categories & Payees from the menu.

2. Click Set Up Tax Categories in the left pane.

3. Click the category you want to describe.

4. Select the Include On Tax Reports check box.

5. Use the Tax Form box to specify the tax form on which this category should be reported.

6. Use the Form Line box to specify the line of the tax form specified in step 5 on which this category should be reported.

7. To keep the books for more than one sole proprietorship, use the Form Copy box to identify each sole proprietorship and Schedule C or C-EZ combination: 1 for the first one, 2 for the second one, and so on.

8. Repeat steps 3 through 7 for each of the business categories you'll work with.

Recording Business Income and Expenses

Once you set up the accounts and categories you need for tracking business income and expenses, you're ready to begin recording the income and expenses.

SEE ALSO

See "Setting Up Bank Accounts" on page 16 for more information about creating an account.

Record Business Income

1. Display the business account's register.

2. Click the Deposit tab, and if necessary, click New.

3. Enter the invoice number if applicable.

4. Enter the deposit date.

5. Enter the customer's name, or select the name from the From field.

6. Enter the amount of the deposit.

7. Click the down arrow in the Category field, and select the category that describes the deposit's income category.

8. Optionally, enter a description of the deposit.

9. Click Enter.

SEE ALSO

See "Timesaving Tips for Entering Transactions" on page 27 for a list of data-entry tricks you can use to speed the process of entering transactions into an account register.

Record a Business Expense

1 Display the business account's register.

2 Click the Withdrawal tab, and if necessary, click New.

3 Enter the check number.

4 Enter the check date.

5 Enter the name of the person or business you're paying, or select it from the Pay To field.

6 Enter the amount of the check.

7 Click the down arrow in the Category field, and select the category that describes the check's expense category.

8 Optionally, enter a description of the check.

9 Click Enter.

11

Preparing for Accounts Receivable Accounting

Although Money isn't really set up to invoice customers and to track the amounts that you've billed to and collected from customers, with a little coercion, you can use Money to keep track of invoices and payments. You just need to set up an accounts receivable account and then use a word processing program to produce the actual invoice.

TIP

Money Business & Personal. *The method which I describe here for tracking accounts receivable works in any version of Money. Note, however, that the Business & Personal version of Money provides a Contact Manager, which lets you track customer invoices. The Business & Personal version of Money also lets you invoice customers.*

Set Up an Accounts Receivable Account

1. Click Accounts on the navigation bar.

2. Click Set Up Accounts in the left pane.

3. Click the Add A New Account hyperlink to start the New Account Wizard.

4. Leave the Held At field empty, and click Next.

5. Select Asset from the list, and click Next.

6. Enter a name for the account so you can recognize it as your accounts receivable account. You could name it simply "Accounts Receivable," for example. Click Next.

7. Enter *0* in the What Is The Asset's Current Value field.

8. Click Next.

9. When Money asks whether you want to associate a loan account with the asset, select the No option and click Finish.

Cash-Basis vs. Accrual-Basis Accounting

Cash-basis accounting counts any checking account deposit as income and any checking account withdrawal as an expense. Cash-basis accounting is commonly employed in small businesses because it's easy to use. But it's usually less accurate than the alternative, accrual-basis accounting, in the way that it measures profits. Accrual-basis accounting counts income when you bill customers and counts expense when you charge or incur bills. The problem with accrual-basis accounting, however, is that to use it, you need to understand double-entry bookkeeping.

Cash-basis accounting counts income when you receive the cash and counts expense when you pay a bill. This might sound correct, but it tends to produce some funny profit measurements. For example, if you're using cash-basis accounting to measure your profits, your profits increase when you delay payment of your bills. And if you're using cash-basis accounting and a customer's check arrives next month instead of this month, your profits for the current month decrease. For example, you can easily increase or decrease your records of profits for the year by simply waiting until January 1 to write a check for something purchased during December or to enter a deposit for a service rendered during December.

Accrual-basis accounting counts income when you bill the customer and counts expense when you charge some amount or incur some expense. Accrual-basis accounting more accurately measures your profits in a given time period, but it's more complicated and more work because you use double-entry bookkeeping. All large companies and most small companies use accrual-basis accounting because it is less susceptible to manipulation and is employed by all auditors and certified public accountants.

11

Recording an Invoice

How you record an invoice depends on the accounting system you use. If you want to use cash-basis accounting, you simply use your accounts receivable account to list your unpaid invoices. If you use accrual-basis accounting, you record an invoice as an increase in the accounts receivable account, and then you record the payment as a transfer from the accounts receivable account to the bank account.

TIP

When cash-basis accounting makes most sense.
Cash-basis accounting, while less accurate for profit measurement, actually makes most sense for small businesses that want to closely watch their cash flows. In effect, by choosing to use cash-basis accounting, you choose cash-flow-measurement accuracy over profit-measurement accuracy.

Record an Invoice with Cash-Basis Accounting

1. Display the accounts receivable account.

2. Click the Increase tab, and if necessary, click New.

3. Enter the invoice date.

4. Enter the name of the customer.

5. Enter the invoice amount.

6. Leave the Category fields empty.

7. Optionally, enter a description of the invoice; for example, a purchase order number.

8. Click Enter.

9. When Money asks whether you're sure you want to leave the Category field empty, click Yes.

TIP

Consider an upgrade. *If your accounting system is sophisticated enough that you require an accounts payable account to track bills as you incur them, you should consider upgrading to a small business accounting program.*

SEE ALSO

See "Adding Business Income and Expense Categories" on page 174 for more information about setting up business income and expense categories.

Record an Invoice with Accrual-Basis Accounting

1. Display the accounts receivable account.

2. Click the Increase tab, and if necessary, click New.

3. Enter the invoice date.

4. Enter the name of the customer.

5. Enter the invoice amount.

6. Use the Category fields to specify an income category. By doing this, you count a customer invoice as income when you bill rather than when you collect.

7. Optionally, enter a description of the invoice; for example, a purchase order number.

8. Click Enter.

Recording a Customer Payment

How you record a customer payment depends on the accounting system you use. To record a customer payment using cash-basis accounting, you first record the customer's check as a deposit in the bank account, and then you record the decrease in the accounts receivable account. To record a customer payment using accrual-basis accounting, you record a deposit in the bank account and transfer the money from the accounts receivable account.

SEE ALSO

See "Recording Business Income and Expenses" on page 176 for more information on how to also record and categorize the customer's check in the business account's register.

Record a Customer Payment with Cash-Basis Accounting

1. Display the accounts receivable account's register.

2. Click the Decrease tab, and if necessary, click New.

3. Enter the payment date.

4. Select the customer's name from the Pay To field.

5. Enter the amount of the check.

6. Leave the Category fields empty.

7. Optionally, enter a description of the check, such as the customer's check number, in the Memo field.

8. Click Enter.

9. Mark the invoice(s) that the customer's check pays and the customer's check as reconciled by right-clicking each transaction and choosing Mark As from the shortcut menu and Reconciled from the submenu.

Mark invoices as paid.

To mark the invoices that the customer's check pays as reconciled, display the accounts receivable account register and right-click the invoice transaction. Then choose Mark As from the shortcut menu and Reconciled from the submenu. Repeat this process for the transfer transaction to mark it as reconciled as well.

Record a Customer Payment with Accrual-Basis Accounting

1. Display the business's bank account register.

2. Click the Deposit tab, and if necessary, click New.

3. Enter the customer's check number.

4. Enter the payment date.

5. Click the down arrow in the From field, and select the name of the customer making the payment.

6. Enter the amount of the check.

7. Enter Transfer in the Category field.

8. Click the down arrow in the Subcategory field, and select the name of the accounts receivable account.

9. Optionally, enter a description of the check in the Memo field.

10. Click Enter.

Monitoring Accounts Receivable

On a regular basis, you need to review your accounts receivable. In particular, you want to watch out for delinquent customer invoices—invoices that should have been paid but haven't been paid. To do this, you can produce a report that summarizes the transactions in the accounts receivable account and sorts the information by customer name.

TIP

Control your report's appearance. *The Customize Report dialog box's Font tab lets you choose a font and point size for your report's information.*

Produce an Accounts Receivable Report

1 Click Reports on the navigation bar.

2 Click Spending Habits in the left pane.

3 Select Account Transactions from the list.

4 Click Go To Report/Chart.

5 Click Customize on the Accounts bar to open the Customize Report dialog box.

6 Click the Rows & Columns tab.

7 Specify which pieces of register information you want to appear on the report.

8 Select Payees from the Subtotal By field.

9 Click the Account tab.

10 Select your accounts receivable account.

If you're using the Memo field to store information such as invoice numbers or check numbers, make sure the Memo check box is selected.

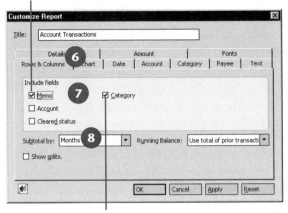

If you aren't using the Category fields when you enter transactions, you can clear the Category check box.

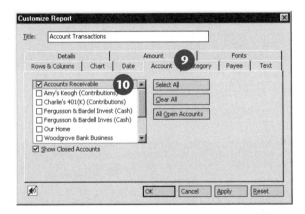

Simplify your reports.
If you're using cash-basis accounting, you can clear the category check box. You're not using this field, so it will only appear blank on your reports anyway.

⑪ Click the Details tab.

⑫ Select Unreconciled Transactions from the Status field.

⑬ Click OK.

11

Setting Up Payroll Accounts to Track Withholdings

Money doesn't provide a payroll feature as such, but it can reduce the work of preparing a payroll. You can use Money, for example, to record and print payroll checks. You can also produce quarterly and yearly payroll reports that you can use to prepare payroll tax returns. The first thing you need to do to begin tracking payroll expenses using Money is to set up payroll liability accounts to track Social Security taxes, Medicare taxes, and federal income tax withholdings.

> **TIP**
>
> **Another way to prepare payroll.** *Many small businesses also use outside payroll service bureaus for preparing their payroll checks and payroll tax returns. Check your local telephone directory for details.*

Set Up Payroll Liability Accounts

① Click Accounts on the navigation bar.

② Click Set Up Accounts in the left pane.

③ Click the Add A New Account hyperlink to start the New Account Wizard.

④ Leave the Held At field empty, and click Next.

⑤ Select Liability from the list of account types, and click Next.

⑥ Enter a name for the liability account. For example, use the names Social Security, Medicare, and Federal Tax to track the different taxes you withhold and owe. Click Next.

⑦ Enter the amount you currently owe for the tax, and click Finish.

⑧ Repeat steps 2 through 7 to set up a separate account for each of the taxes.

New Account

What do you want to name this account?

Name: Social Security ⑥

< Back | Next > | Cancel

New Account

What's the opening value of this account?

Enter the ending cash balance from your last statement (if you have one). To start your records from an earlier date, use the balance from the earlier statement. Later, you can enter all transactions from that date until now.

Note: If you don't know the exact balance, estimate. You can change it later.

How much do you owe on this account?

153.00 ⑦

What is the currency for this account?

US Dollar

< Back | Finish | Cancel

Payroll Tax Reporting Requirements

To meet the federal payroll tax and reporting requirements, your first step is to get an employer tax identification number. This number is equivalent to your personal Social Security number—it identifies you as an employer and is used by the government to track transactions relating specifically to your responsibilities as an employer. To get an employer tax identification number, contact the Internal Revenue Service (IRS) and ask for an SS-4 form. This form, which is very simple to fill out, tells the IRS you want to hire an employee.

Once you request an employer tax identification number, the IRS knows you're an employer and sends you the federal tax deposit coupons you use to remit the money withheld from employees' paychecks. And, at the end of the quarter and the end of the year, the IRS sends you the payroll tax returns you need to complete: the end-of-quarter 941 return to report the wages you've paid for the quarter and the end-of-year 940 return to report any federal unemployment tax you owe.

The IRS also sends you a copy of the *Employer's Tax Guide.* This booklet, which is sometimes called a "Circular E," tells you how much federal income tax, Social Security tax, and Medicare tax you're supposed to withhold from an employee's paycheck. You need this booklet to prepare payroll checks. Watch for it, and don't lose it.

State and Local Payroll Tax and Reporting Requirements

Your state also has payroll tax and reporting requirements that you need to meet. States, for example, require employers to pay unemployment insurance and disability insurance, also known as *workman's compensation.* Most states have a state income tax that you, as an employer, need to withhold from employee checks and then remit to the state. You may also have local county or city payroll tax reporting requirements.

I can't give you precise instructions for meeting state and local payroll tax reporting requirements because they vary from state to state. Contact the state or local employment tax office, and tell them you are hiring an employee or several employees. The office will put you on its list of employers. Typically, as soon as this happens, you get instructions on what you're supposed to do. And you periodically get payroll tax returns you're supposed to fill out and return. (End-of-quarter payroll tax returns are common, for example.)

Other Employee Reporting Requirements

In addition to the payroll tax and reporting requirements described in the preceding paragraphs, employers are also required to perform other tasks. The Immigration and Naturalization Service, for example, requires employers to verify that their employees are U.S. citizens, Permanent Residents, or have a work visa. Some states have special reporting requirements, for example, to help track down parents who aren't making court-ordered child support payments. And there are often other special reporting requirements as well.

11

Setting Up Payroll Categories

Once you've set up your payroll liability accounts, you need to set up several new payroll expense categories. Specifically, you need to set up a category called "Payroll" and several subcategories within this category to track your taxes and payroll expenses.

TIP

Which categories are tax-related? *Tax-related categories appear in the Tax Software Setup window with an X in the Tax field. Make sure that all tax-related categories have a tax form and line assigned to them in the Tax Form and Line fields. See "Identifying the Tax Treatment of a Category" on page 175 for more information on assigning categories a line on a particular tax form.*

Set Up the Payroll Expense Category

1 Click More on the navigation bar, and then choose Categories & Payees from the menu.

2 Click Categories in the left pane.

3 Click New.

4 Click the Create A New Category option button, and click Next.

5 Enter the new category name as Payroll in the Name field.

6 Click the Expense option button, and click Next.

7 Select Other Expense from the list.

8 Click Finish.

Which payroll subcategories you use. *You'll probably want to create the following subcategories under Payroll: Gross Wages, Employer's Social Security, and Employer's Medicare. You also need to create categories for any other payroll taxes or expenses you pay, such as for state disability insurance and any retirement plans.*

Set Up Payroll Expense Subcategories

1. Click More on the navigation bar, and then choose Categories & Payees from the menu.

2. Click Categories in the left pane.

3. Select Payroll from the Categories field.

4. Click New.

5. Click the Add A Subcategory To Payroll option button, and click Next.

6. Enter a name for the new category in the Name field. For example, use the name Gross Wages to track gross wages.

7. Click Next, and click Finish.

8. Repeat steps 3 through 7 to add the other payroll subcategories.

Writing Payroll Checks

Once you've set up the payroll accounts and payroll categories you need, preparing a payroll check is a snap. You just need to figure out how much you're supposed to withhold for the employee based on the information the employee provided on his or her W-4 form and the tables listed in the current *Employer's Tax Guide.* Then you enter the amounts you calculate in the Split Transaction dialog box.

TIP

Payroll preparation instructions for household employees. *The payroll preparation instructions provided here not only work for business employees. They work for household employees—such as childcare workers—too.*

Record a Check to an Employee

① Display the business bank account's register, click the Withdrawal tab, and if necessary, click New.

② Enter the check number, date, and Pay To information in the usual way.

③ Click Split.

④ Describe the gross wages on the first line of the Split Transaction dialog box by specifying the Category as Payroll and the Subcategory as Gross Wages. Enter the gross wages in the Amount field.

⑤ Describe the federal income taxes withheld from the paycheck on the second line by specifying the Category as Transfer and the Subcategory as Federal Tax. Enter the amount in the Amount field.

⑥ Describe the Social Security taxes paid by the employee through withholding on the third line by specifying the Category as Transfer and the Subcategory as Social Security. Enter the amount in the Amount field.

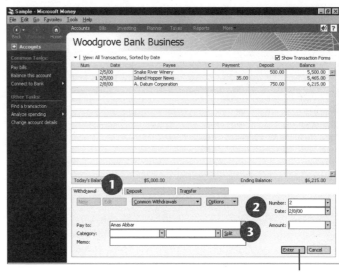

Click Enter to record the payroll check in the register.

Click Done to close the Split Transaction box.

Scroll down to enter or see the employer's share of the Medicare taxes.

TIP

How Social Security and Medicare taxes work. *Both the employer and employee pay a Medicare tax equal to 1.45 percent of the employee's gross wages. The employer and employees both also typically pay a Social Security tax equal to 6.2 percent of the employee's gross wages.*

TIP

Make tax deposits with the IRS. *To record the check you use to pay the IRS for some payroll tax you owe, just write the check for whatever amount you owe. Then record the check as a transfer to the liability account.*

7 Describe the Medicare taxes paid by the employee through withholding on the fourth line by specifying the Category as Transfer and the Subcategory as Medicare. Enter the amount in the Amount field.

8 Enter the employer's matching Social Security expense on the fifth line by specifying the Category as Payroll and the Subcategory as Employer's Social Security.

9 Enter the amount of money owed the federal government for Social Security tax on the sixth line by specifying the Category as Transfer and the Subcategory as Social Security.

10 Enter the employer's matching Medicare taxes on the seventh line by specifying the Category as Payroll and the Subcategory as Employer's Medicare.

11 Enter the amount of money owed the federal government for this Medicare tax on the eighth line by specifying the Category as Transfer and the Subcategory as Medicare.

11

Preparing W-2 and W-3 Forms

The other payroll task you must complete is the annual preparation of W-2 forms and the W-3 form. You complete a W-2 for each employee to summarize the gross pay earned over the year and the taxes withheld over the year. The W-3 summarizes all the W-2s. Although Money won't print these forms for you, you can use it to calculate the needed information and display it in a report.

TIP

Stock up on forms. *You can typically acquire blank W-2 and W-3 forms at the local office supplies store.*

Produce a Payroll Transaction Report

1. Click Reports on the navigation bar.

2. Click Spending Habits in the left pane.

3. Double-click Who Is Getting My Money in the list.

4. Click Customize to open the Customize Report dialog box.

5. Change the report's title by clicking the Title field and typing Employee Wages Summary.

6. Click the Rows & Columns tab.

7. Click the down arrow in the Rows field, and select Subcategories from the list.

8. Click the down arrow in the Columns field, and select Payees from the list.

9. Enter *0* in the Combine All Values Under X % Of Total field.

10. Click the Date tab.

11. Use the Range options to tell Money for which year you want to prepare the W-2s and W-3.

See "Printing Reports" on pages 64–65 for more information on printing reports.

Switch to report. *If Money initially displays a chart instead of a report, click the Report button. The Report button shows a report icon and appears in the lower left corner of the window.*

Use for quarterly and annual tax returns. *You should also be able to use the Employee Wages Summary report to prepare the quarterly and annual payroll tax returns.*

12 Click the Category tab.

13 Click Clear All.

14 Select the Payroll expense category and the Payroll subcategories from the list, and click OK.

15 Click OK to produce the Employee Wages Summary report.

16 Print the report by choosing Print from the File menu. With the help of the IRS instructions, you should be able to use the information provided by your printed report to complete the W-2 and W-3 forms.

Measuring Profits

There are many reasons for owning or operating a small business. Autonomy, for one, or maybe just plain fun. But for a business to survive, the business must produce profits. Accordingly, on a regular basis, you need to calculate whether you're making a profit. As long as you've been collecting information about your income and expenses, it's very easy to produce a profit and loss statement using Money.

TIP

Get information on your competitors' profits. *Both Robert Morris & Associates and Standard & Poor's publish financial statistics on a variety of businesses. The data is arranged by size of business and by standard industry classification, or SIC, codes. You can obtain these publications at your local library.*

Produce a Profit and Loss Statement

1. Click Reports on the navigation bar.

2. Click Spending Habits in the left pane.

3. Select Income vs. Spending from the list.

4. Click Go To Report/Chart.

5. Click Customize to open the Customize Report dialog box.

6. Change the report's title by clicking the Title field and typing *Profit and Loss Statement*.

7. Click the Date tab.

8. Use the Range options to tell Money for which time period you want to measure profits.

9 Click the Category tab.

10 Select the business income and expense categories that you want to appear on your Profit and Loss Statement from the list.

11 Click OK to produce the Profit and Loss Statement.

12 Print the statement by choosing Print from the File menu.

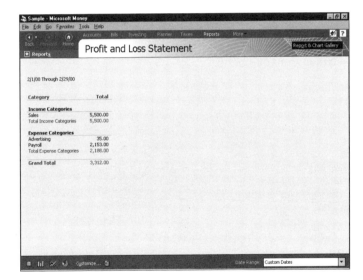

Measuring Cash Flow

Over the long haul, a business can't survive without profits, but cash flow is more important in the short run. To make it through the next month or quarter, for example, you need to have enough cash to pay all your bills and to make any needed investments in new machinery or equipment.

TIP

Cash flow statements for cash-basis businesses. *If you use cash-basis accounting for tracking your income and expenses, your profit and loss statement and cash flow statement may look very similar.*

Produce a Monthly Cash Flow Statement

1 Click Reports on the navigation bar.

2 Click Spending Habits in the left pane.

3 Select Monthly Cash Flow from the list.

4 Click Go To Report/Chart.

5 Click Customize to open the Customize Report dialog box.

6 Click the Date tab.

7 Use the Range options to tell Money for which time period you want to measure cash flow.

8 Click the Account tab.

9 Click Select All to make sure that transfers to and from all your accounts are included.

Why does my cash flow differ from my profit? *If you record your business income when you deposit customer payments and you record your business expenses when you write checks, you use cash-basis accounting. In this case, your profit and loss statement will closely resemble your cash flow statement. The only differences will result from account transfers to and from your bank accounts. These transfers appear on cash flow statements because they involve cash moving in or out of a bank account. But they don't appear on profit and loss statements.*

10 Click the Category tab.

11 Select the business income and expense categories that you want to appear on your Cash Flow Statement from the list.

12 Click OK to produce the Cash Flow Statement.

13 Print the statement by choosing Print from the File menu.

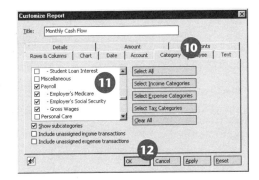

Measuring Net Worth

With a balance sheet, you tally your assets and liabilities and calculate the difference between these two amounts to get your business's net worth. A balance sheet provides several pieces of useful information. It lets you assess the liquidity of your business, helps you calculate return on investment figures, and provides information you need to determine how fast you can grow your business.

TIP

Balance sheet "as of" dates.
Businesses usually measure their net worth at the end of the month, quarter, and year—and at the end of any other period for which profits are calculated using a profit and loss statement.

Produce a Balance Sheet

1 Click Reports on the navigation bar.

2 Click What I Have in the left pane.

3 Select Account Balances from the list.

4 Click Go To Report/Chart.

5 Click Customize to open the Customize Report dialog box.

6 Change the report's title by clicking in the Title field and typing *Balance Sheet*.

7 Click the Rows & Columns tab.

8 Use the Show Balances As Of field to specify the date for which you want the account balance calculated.

How fast can I grow my business? *In general, you can grow your business only as fast as you can grow your net worth. For example, if you want to grow your business by 25 percent annually, you need to grow your net worth by 25 percent annually. Because a small business usually increases its net worth only by reinvesting profits, however, these reinvested profits limit your growth. For example, if reinvested profits as a percentage of net worth equal 20 percent, you can only grow your business by 20 percent.*

How to interpret the balance sheet. *A general rule of thumb is that the sum of your cash, accounts receivable, and any investments should at least be equal to your short-term debts. Your short-term debts include liabilities you have to pay in the coming year, any amounts you now owe employees or creditors, business credit-card balances, and the loan principal payments you'll make over the next year. You should be able to get all this information from your balance sheet.*

9 Click the Account tab.

10 Click Clear All, and then individually select each of the business accounts that should be summarized on the Balance Sheet.

11 Click OK to produce the Balance Sheet.

12 Print the Balance Sheet by choosing Print from the File menu.

11

Preparing Income Tax Returns

If you use Money for your business bookkeeping, you want to be able to produce reports that summarize the required information for your federal and state income tax returns. If you're just starting a business, you'll first need to know which form you'll be using. The following table lists the standard federal income tax forms that businesses file.

FORM	USE IT TO REPORT
1040 Schedule C	Profit or loss from a sole proprietorship
1040 Schedule C-EZ	Profit or loss from a small sole proprietorship
1040 Schedule F	Income and expenses from farming
1040 Schedule SE	Tax due on income from self-employment
Form 1120	Income and expenses for a corporation
Form 1120A	Income and expenses for a corporation with gross receipts of less that $500,000
Form 1120S	Annual information for an S-corporation
Form 1065	Annual information for a partnership

You can download the most recent copies of these forms and schedules, along with the instructions that go with them, from the Internal Revenue Service web site at *http://www.irs.ustreas.gov*.

The figure on the next page shows an example of Schedule C from Form 1040 for 1997 and 1998. If you're a sole proprietor, you can use the income and expenses listed on this form as a basis for your categories in Money. If a more recent form is available when you set up your categories in Money, however, you should use it. Don't worry if the most recent form you can get is from the previous year. Forms aren't finalized until late in the year, but you need to track your income and expenses from the beginning of the year.

Part I Income

1. Gross receipts or sales. **Caution:** *If this income was reported to you on Form W-2 and the "Statutory employee" box on that form was checked, see page C-3 and check here* ▶ ☐ | **1** | |
2. Returns and allowances . . . . | **2** | |
3. Subtract line 2 from line 1 . . . . | **3** | |
4. Cost of goods sold (from line 42 on page 2) . . . . | **4** | |
5. **Gross profit.** Subtract line 4 from line 3 . . . . | **5** | |
6. Other income, including Federal and state gasoline or fuel tax credit or refund (see page C-3) . . . | **6** | |
7. **Gross income.** Add lines 5 and 6 . . . . ▶ | **7** | |

Part II Expenses. Enter expenses for business use of your home **only** on line 30.

8 Advertising	**8**		**19** Pension and profit-sharing plans	**19**	
9 Bad debts from sales or services (see page C-3) . .	**9**		**20** Rent or lease (see page C-5):		
			a Vehicles, machinery, and equipment .	**20a**	
10 Car and truck expenses (see page C-3)	**10**		**b** Other business property . .	**20b**	
11 Commissions and fees . .	**11**		**21** Repairs and maintenance . .	**21**	
12 Depletion	**12**		**22** Supplies (not included in Part III) .	**22**	
13 Depreciation and section 179 expense deduction (not included in Part III) (see page C-4) . .	**13**		**23** Taxes and licenses	**23**	
			24 Travel, meals, and entertainment:		
			a Travel	**24a**	
14 Employee benefit programs (other than on line 19) . . .	**14**		**b** Meals and entertainment .		
15 Insurance (other than health) .	**15**		**c** Enter 50% of line 24b subject to limitations (see page C-6) .		
16 Interest:					
a Mortgage (paid to banks, etc.) .	**16a**		**d** Subtract line 24c from line 24b	**24d**	
b Other	**16b**		**25** Utilities	**25**	
17 Legal and professional services	**17**		**26** Wages (less employment credits) .	**26**	
18 Office expense	**18**		**27** Other expenses (from line 48 on page 2)	**27**	

11

Index

assets, *continued*

graphs. *See* charts

help, online, 11
home. *See also* mortgages
    calculating loan interest, 105
    estimating affordability,
        84–85
    inventorying assets, 90–91,
        103
    as real estate investment, 135
    setting up asset account, 100,
        102–3
    setting up loan account,
        104–5
    tips for recordkeeping, 102–3
home banking. *See* online
    services
home equity loans, 95
Home Inventory worksheet,
    90–91, 103
Home Page, Money, 10
Home Worksheet, 84–85

importing Quicken files, 9
income, recording, 19, 20–21
income taxes. *See* taxes
Income *vs.* Spending report,
    148
installing Microsoft Money, 6
insurance, keeping asset lists
    for, 103

interest
    accrued interest, 132
    recording bond interest, 129
Internal Revenue Service
    how long to keep records, 66
    list of Schedule C categories,
        201
    payroll reporting require-
        ments, 187
Internet. *See also* online
    services
    financial web sites, 169, 170,
        171
    mailing lists, 169
    newsgroups, 168
    online quotes, 119–21
    researching investments,
        168–69
    setting up connection,
        152–53
    Web Express, 170
Internet Explorer, 152
inventory, home, 90–91, 103
investment accounts
    recording commissions, 123,
        124
    recording distributions, 125
    recording dividends, 125
    recording lot price, 116
    recording other income and
        expenses, 127
    recording purchases, 122–23
    recording sales, 124
    reports, 55, 125, 148
    setting up, 114–15
    updating prices, 120
Investment Portfolio window,
    118

investments. *See also* bonds;
        investment accounts;
        real estate
    cash accounts, 115
    for college savings, 74–75
    describing portfolio, 116–17
    loans as, 105
    obtaining quotes online,
        119–21
    researching on the Internet,
        168–69
    updating long-term records,
        124
    when to track in Money, 113,
        115
invoices, recording, 180–81
IRAs, 95
IRS. *See* Internal Revenue
    Service

Keogh Plans, 95

landscape orientation, 64
liability accounts
    entering payments, 107
    vs. loan accounts, 106
    for payroll, 186
    setting up, 106
Lifetime Planner, 70–71, 74
lists. *See* categories; payees

loan accounts. *See also* liability
        accounts
    creating, 104–5
    fixing account balance errors,
        108–9
    vs. liability accounts, 106
Loan Planner worksheet, 88–89
loans. *See also* credit cards;
        mortgages
    calculation variables, 105
    college loans, 77
    comparing using Loan
        Planner worksheet,
        88–89
    creating accounts, 104–5
    entering interest rate, 105
    home equity loans, 95
    interest calculations, 105
lots, stock, 116, 124

mailing lists, 169
margin interest, recording, 127
Memo field, 47. *See also*
        comments
Microsoft Excel, exporting
        Money reports to, 67
Microsoft Money
    creating files, 8
    Currency Converter, 26
    exiting, 13
    Home Page, 10
    installing, 6
    online help, 11
    online quotes, 119–21
    opening files, 8
    Planning Center, defined, 69

taxes, *continued*

estimating, 92–93
list of Schedule C categories, 201
payroll reporting requirements, 187
preparing returns, 200–201
state and local, 187
tax-related categories, 175, 188, 201
tax-related reports, 55, 58, 59
tips for saving on, 94–95
Tax Estimator worksheet, 92–93
technical support, Microsoft Money, 171
text files, exporting Money reports as, 67
transaction forms, 19, 27
transactions. *See also* account register; investments; real estate; small business
deleting, 35
editing, 35
entering, 19–23, 27
fictitious, 41
finding, 36–37
forgotten, 41
lost, 36–37
recurring, 32–33
replacing information, 37
splitting, 29
tips for entering, 27
transfers, recording, 28
tuition, college. *See* college
Tuition Savings Calculator, 87
.txt files, 67

Update Details window, 18
upgrading Microsoft Money, 7
U.S. savings bonds, tracking, 115

voiding checks, 35

Wall Street Journal, 169
Web Express, 170
web sites, 169, 170, 171
    See also Internet
W-2 forms, 192–93
W-3 forms, 192–93
What I Have reports, 55
What I Owe reports, 55
withdrawals, recording, 22–23
withholding, 186, 187
worksheets
Home Inventory worksheet, 90–91, 103
Home Worksheet, 84–85
World Wide Web, 169, 170, 171. *See also* Internet

year-end reports, 58, 59

zero-coupon bonds, 129

The manuscript for this book was prepared and submitted to Microsoft Press in electronic form. Text files were prepared using Microsoft Word 2000. Pages were composed by Stephen L. Nelson, Inc., using PageMaker for Windows, with text in Stone Sans and display type in Stone Serif and Stone Serif Semibold. Composed pages were delivered to the printer as electronic prepress files.

Cover Designer
Girvin | Branding & Design

Graphic Layout
Stefan Knorr

Indexer
Julie Kawabata

See clearly— *now!*

Here's the remarkable, *visual* way to quickly find answers about the powerfully integrated features of the Microsoft® Office 2000 applications. Microsoft Press AT A GLANCE books let you focus on particular tasks and show you, with clear, numbered steps, the easiest way to get them done right now. Put Office 2000 to work today, with AT A GLANCE learning solutions, made by Microsoft.

- MICROSOFT OFFICE 2000 PROFESSIONAL AT A GLANCE
- MICROSOFT WORD 2000 AT A GLANCE
- MICROSOFT EXCEL 2000 AT A GLANCE
- MICROSOFT POWERPOINT® 2000 AT A GLANCE
- MICROSOFT ACCESS 2000 AT A GLANCE
- MICROSOFT FRONTPAGE® 2000 AT A GLANCE
- MICROSOFT PUBLISHER 2000 AT A GLANCE
- MICROSOFT OFFICE 2000 SMALL BUSINESS AT A GLANCE
- MICROSOFT PHOTODRAW® 2000 AT A GLANCE
- MICROSOFT INTERNET EXPLORER 5 AT A GLANCE
- MICROSOFT OUTLOOK® 2000 AT A GLANCE

mspress.microsoft.com

Stay in the *running* for maximum *productivity.*

These are *the* answer books for business users of Microsoft® Office 2000. They are packed with everything from quick, clear instructions for new users to comprehensive answers for power users—the authoritative reference to keep by your computer and use every day. THE RUNNING SERIES—learning solutions made by Microsoft.

- RUNNING MICROSOFT EXCEL 2000
- RUNNING MICROSOFT OFFICE 2000 PREMIUM
- RUNNING MICROSOFT OFFICE 2000 PROFESSIONAL
- RUNNING MICROSOFT OFFICE 2000 SMALL BUSINESS
- RUNNING MICROSOFT WORD 2000
- RUNNING MICROSOFT POWERPOINT® 2000
- RUNNING MICROSOFT ACCESS 2000
- RUNNING MICROSOFT INTERNET EXPLORER 5
- RUNNING MICROSOFT FRONTPAGE® 2000
- RUNNING MICROSOFT OUTLOOK® 2000

Microsoft®

mspress.microsoft.com

Step up!

STEP BY STEP books provide quick and easy self-training—to help you learn to use the powerful word processing, spreadsheet, database, presentation, communication, and Internet components of Microsoft Office 2000—both individually and together. The easy-to-follow lessons present clear objectives and real-world business examples, with numerous screen shots and illustrations. Put Office 2000 to work today, with STEP BY STEP learning solutions, made by Microsoft.

- MICROSOFT® OFFICE PROFESSIONAL 8-IN-1 STEP BY STEP
- MICROSOFT WORD 2000 STEP BY STEP
- MICROSOFT EXCEL 2000 STEP BY STEP
- MICROSOFT POWERPOINT® 2000 STEP BY STEP
- MICROSOFT INTERNET EXPLORER 5 STEP BY STEP
- MICROSOFT PUBLISHER 2000 STEP BY STEP
- MICROSOFT ACCESS 2000 STEP BY STEP
- MICROSOFT FRONTPAGE 2000 STEP BY STEP
- MICROSOFT OUTLOOK 2000 STEP BY STEP

Microsoft Press® products are available worldwide wherever quality computer books are sold. For more information, contact your book or computer retailer, software reseller, or local Microsoft Sales Office, or visit our Web site at mspress.microsoft.com. To locate your nearest source for Microsoft Press products, or to order directly, call 1-800-MSPRESS in the U.S. (in Canada, call 1-800-268-2222).

Prices and availability dates are subject to change.

mspress.microsoft.com

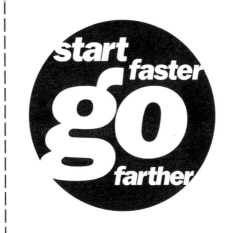

Register Today!

Return this
Microsoft® Money 2000 At a Glance
registration card today

Microsoft®Press
mspress.microsoft.com

OWNER REGISTRATION CARD   0-7356-0811-3

Microsoft® Money 2000 At a Glance

_____   _____   _____
FIRST NAME   MIDDLE INITIAL   LAST NAME

_____
INSTITUTION OR COMPANY NAME

_____
ADDRESS

_____

_____   _____   _____
CITY   STATE   ZIP

                                                                ( )
_____   _____
E-MAIL ADDRESS   PHONE NUMBER

U.S. and Canada addresses only. Fill in information above and mail postage-free.
Please mail only the bottom half of this page.

For information about Microsoft Press®

products, visit our Web site at

mspress.microsoft.com

Microsoft®*Press*

BUSINESS REPLY MAIL

FIRST-CLASS MAIL   PERMIT NO. 108   REDMOND WA

POSTAGE WILL BE PAID BY ADDRESSEE

MICROSOFT PRESS
PO BOX 97017
REDMOND, WA 98073-9830